Pricing Money

Pricing Money

**A Beginner's Guide to Money,
Bonds, Futures and Swaps**

J. D. A. Wiseman

JOHN WILEY & SONS, LTD

Chichester · New York · Weinheim · Brisbane · Singapore · Toronto

Copyright © 1998 by John Wiley & Sons, Ltd, The Atrium, Southern Gate,
Chichester, West Sussex PO19 8SQ, England
Telephone (+44) 1243 779777

Email (for orders and customer service enquiries): cs-books@wiley.co.uk
Visit our Home Page www.wileyeurope.com or www.wiley.com

Reprinted September 2006, May 2007, February 2008

Other Wiley Editorial Offices

John Wiley & Sons Inc., 111 River Street, Hoboken, NJ 07030, USA

Jossey-Bass, 989 Market Street, San Francisco, CA 94103-1741, USA

Wiley-VCH Verlag GmbH, Boschstr. 12, D-69469 Weinheim, Germany

John Wiley & Sons Australia Ltd, 33 Park Road, Milton, Queensland 4064, Australia

John Wiley & Sons (Asia) Pte Ltd, 2 Clementi Loop #02-01, Jin Xing Distripark, Singapore
129809

John Wiley & Sons (Canada) Ltd, 22 Worcester Road, Etobicoke, Ontario M9W 1L1

Wiley also publishes its books in a variety of electronic formats. Some content that appears in
print may not be available in electronic books.

Library of Congress Cataloging-in-Publication Data

Wiseman, J. D. A.
   Pricing money : a beginner's guide to money, bonds, futures, and swaps / J. D. A. Wiseman.
      p. cm.
   ISBN 0–471–48700–7
      1. Money market. 2. Bonds. 3. Futures. 4. Options (Finance) 5. Swaps (Finance) 6.
Foreign exchange. I. Title.

   HG226.W57 2001
   332.63´2–dc21   2001026498

British Library Cataloguing in Publication Data

A catalogue record for this book is available from the British Library

ISBN 978–0–471–48700–5 (pbk)

Typeset in 10/12pt Times by Deerpark Publishing Services, Ireland

To AFM, RML and SAP

Contents

CONTENTS

CONTENTS

CONTENTS

CONTENTS

Preface

A company borrows some money from its bank for two years at an interest rate of 5%. This transaction contains interest-rate risk and credit risk. It might be that the bank is willing to hold one or both of these risks; or it might be that their nature or size prevents the bank from holding either. Financial markets allow the constituent risks in such a transaction to be priced independently, and for those risks to be recombined into forms for which a willing home can be found. Thus the financial markets allow borrowers to raise funds and investors to purchase assets. The various financial instruments enable investors, borrowers and intermediaries to price and transfer different combinations of risk.

During my eight years as an analyst in the financial markets, other researchers and I taught many new colleagues about finance. *Pricing Money* has grown out of those lectures and tutorials, and describes the basics of the trading of interest rates, including deposits, bonds, futures, swaps, options and foreign exchange. In general, these instruments are well designed for their tasks, and this book emphasises the purpose of each of their features.

Pricing Money should be read by those starting employment in finance, and by those hoping to be employed in finance – consider reading it before rather than after the interview. It will also be useful to those employed in non-financial roles within financial institutions, such as computer programmers, accountants, lawyers, and also to civil servants, corporate treasurers and the interested layman. However, it is a beginner's book, with few equations, and avoids encyclopedic listings of every detail. Rather, it gives context to those lists that can be found elsewhere. Some of my proof-readers have even said that they want a copy for their spouse: 'Had a nice day dear? Doing what?' to which the answer should be 'This'.

Pricing Money is divided into two parts. Part 1 is a beginner's toolkit, containing a summary of the basics of interest rate trading: what is traded, who trades it and why. Part 2 goes into more detail and assumes proficiency with Part 1.

J. D. A. Wiseman
London, April 2001
www.jdawiseman.com

Acknowledgements

A number of institutions have kindly allowed me to quote their words. Specifications of futures contracts are taken with the permission of the exchanges: the London International Financial Futures Exchange (LIFFE), the Chicago Board of Trade (CBoT), and the COMEX division of the New York Mercantile Exchange (NYMEX). The specification of Libor is quoted with the permission of the British Bankers' Association. The screen prints on non-government issuance are reproduced with the permission of International Insider; and the specifications of some legal terms are taken from the Recommendations of the International Primary Markets Association. Numerical data for the charts and examples were kindly provided by Credit Suisse First Boston and J. P. Morgan, and the prices of the 2001 gilts by the UK Debt Management Office.

Pricing Money has greatly benefited from the attention of many proof-readers, who have checked for clarity and accuracy, as well as more humdrum typographical errors. These include Richard Armes, David Bakstein, Fiona Brayshaw, Mike Cloherty, Martin Cross, Larry Dyer, Emily Eimer, Simon Gandy, Thomas Green, Ben Gurney, Clare Hantrais, Shahid Ikram, Jeanine Isaac, Alan James, Ten Jia-Mang, Peter Kasprowicz, Tracy Kingsley-Daniells, David Leddy, Gerald Levenson, James Macgillivray, Lily Malin, Laura-Jane Mason, Kamran Moghadam, Richard Moore, Shahzad Mughal, Louise Pitt, Joe Prendergast, Chris Tuffey, Nicolas Vassiliadis, Neale Vincent, Diana Vollmerhausen, Sabrina Weyeneth, Adam Wiseman, Oliver Wiseman, Richard Wiseman, Shirley Wright, Yasuhiro Yoshie and Maarten Zuurmond. Particular thanks goes to William Porter for his

ACKNOWLEDGEMENTS

thorough checking and researching of various corrections, and to Edward Wynn for his detailed attention to my too-numerous linguistic errors.

At this point it is traditional to state that further errors doubtless remain, and that they are the fault of the author. They are: the buck stops here.

Part 1

A Beginner's Toolkit

Chapter 1

Money markets

What is money?

Let us say the publisher of this book owes me, the author, royalties of £100. The publisher sends me a cheque (a check in the US) for £100. But a cheque is not money; a cheque merely instructs a bank to pay. The publisher banks with NatWest, a large UK high-street (commercial) bank, and it is on this bank that the cheque is drawn. I pay the cheque into my account at HSBC. My publisher's account at NatWest is lowered by £100, and my account at HSBC is increased by £100. But how does NatWest pay HSBC?

Both NatWest and HSBC have accounts at the Bank of England (BoE). HSBC is owed £100 by NatWest, and requests payment; in response NatWest sends a payment instruction to the BoE. This instruction causes NatWest's account at the BoE to be lowered by £100, and that of HSBC to be increased by £100. One bank has paid the other; the whole transaction is now complete.

This money on account at the central bank is real money; the other versions are merely promises to pay real money. For most purposes we talk loosely of cash or money, but when the distinction is important we refer to *central-bank money*. True money,

3

more properly called *final money*, can take one of only two forms: physical cash, which is rarely used in wholesale financial markets, and central-bank money. Money on account with a commercial bank is not final money; it is merely a promise to pay.

Although the above example described a small payment, the mechanics described are actually more typical of a large payment. Small payments tend to be batched together and netted, so that if HSBC and NatWest each owe the other, only the difference is transmitted. High-street banks, always keen to reduce their costs, care greatly about the detailed mechanics of small payments, but as this book is about the wholesale financial markets, we leave these details unstated.

Exactly the same principle applies in currencies other than British pounds, but in some there are minor complications. The US central bank, the Federal Reserve System (the Fed), is divided into a number of regional reserve banks; money at any of these regional reserve banks is final money. In general, most banks use an account at the Federal Reserve Bank of New York to settle US dollar activity in the wholesale financial markets. The European Central Bank (ECB) is part of the European System of Central Banks, which includes the Bundesbank (Germany's national central bank), the Banque de France, the Banca d'Italia, and others. Money at any one of the eurozone's National Central Banks (NCBs) is final money. But these are merely details.

In summary the legal definition of money is money on account at the central bank. Any other form of money is really just a promise to pay central-bank money.

Why there is a money market?

To avoid the difficulties of multiple but linked central banks, we return to the example in sterling (a synonym for British pounds), but now assume that the payment was for £100 million. NatWest has reduced its client's account by £100 million, and instructed the BoE to pay the same sum from its account to that of HSBC, and when the confirmation arrives, HSBC increases its client's account by the same amount.

That done, NatWest has £100 million less than it did in its account at the BoE, and HSBC has the same amount more. NatWest now needs to find £100 million, and HSBC has £100 million that is surplus to its immediate requirements. A natural course of action would be for HSBC to lend NatWest the money at an interest rate agreed between the two.

Thus the key purpose of an interbank deposit market, a money market, is to offset the payment system. When customers pay money into their accounts, the bank will want a return on that money. To get that return it will lend the money to other customers or to other banks. And hence, in every currency of relevance to financial markets, banks lend money to each other.

```
CHF  DEPOSITS
O/N  2.60-3.10
T/N  2.83-3.08
S/N  2.83-3.08
1/W  2.88-3.13
2/W  2.88-3.13
1/M  3.27-3.42
2/M  3.28-3.43
3/M  3.30-3.45
6/M  3.38-3.53
9/M  3.42-3.57
12/  3.50-3.65
```

When one bank lends another money, it will be at an agreed interest rate, and for repayment on an agreed maturity. Typical maturities for interbank money range from 1 day for *overnight* money to 6 months, and even out to 1 year, though with much less active trading in the longer maturities. The money market is so important that many banks maintain screens showing the latest prices at which they are willing to borrow and lend. The figure shows a copy of prices for Swiss-franc deposits, as published by Credit Suisse First Boston (CSFB), a large Swiss investment bank, late in the morning of 30 November 2000. At this time CSFB was willing to accept 3-month Swiss-franc deposits at a rate of 3.30%, and to lend Swiss francs to other high-quality banks for the same period at a rate of 3.45%. CSFB was *making a market* in these deposits, *bidding* for 3-month funds at 3.30%, and *offering* 3-month funds at 3.45%. The intention of such market-making is to borrow some at 3.30%, lend some at 3.45%, and keep the 0.15% difference, the *bid-offer spread*, as profit.

Choosing a maturity

Let us say that Goldman Sachs, an American investment bank, needs to borrow Swiss francs for 6 months. One course of action would be for Goldman Sachs to borrow them for 6 months from CSFB at the screen price of 3.53%.

But there are alternatives. For example, Goldman Sachs could borrow the money for only 3 months (at the rate of 3.45%), and after 3 months reborrow the money. Why do this? To have the same cost as a 6-month loan, the reborrowing would have to be at 3.58%. This should make intuitive sense; 3.53%, the 6-month rate, is close to the average of 3.45% and 3.58%, the rates for the first and second 3-month periods.

So, if Goldman Sachs thinks that in 3 months' time the cost of 3-month money will be less than 3.58%, then it would be cheaper overall for Goldman Sachs to borrow now for 3 months at 3.45%, and then in 3 months to reborrow at the rate then prevailing. Of course, if Goldman Sachs thinks that in 3 months' time the cost of borrowing Swiss francs for 3 months is likely to be higher than 3.58%, it should borrow for the entire 6-month period now.

So the *breakeven* cost of 3-month money in 3 months' time is 3.58%. This is said to be the *forward price*. The current price, also known as the *spot price*, of 3-month money is 3.45%; the

3-month forward price of 3-month money is +0.13% over spot. Market prices are implying that Swiss short-term interest rates are rising.

Goldman Sachs has more choices. If it believes that rates are unlikely to rise, then it might be cheapest to borrow for 1 day, and reborrow the money each subsequent day. Or if it thinks that rates are about to rise to very high levels, perhaps the best course would be to borrow money for 1 year (at 3.65%), and in 6 months' time to lend these Swiss francs at the then-prevailing rate, hopefully much higher. No matter which view it takes, by choosing to borrow money at one maturity rather than another, Goldman Sachs is implicitly expressing an opinion on the future path of short-term rates. That opinion is measured—and can only be measured— against the current forward prices.

Exactly the same reasoning applies to an industrial corporation that needs to borrow Swiss francs for 6 months. It cannot avoid some form of implicit speculation; by choosing to borrow at one maturity rather than another, it is taking a view on the future path of interest rates, and that view should be measured against the market's forward prices.

Repo

Let us return to our example, in which HSBC has lent NatWest £100 million, for let us say 3 months. After 3 months, NatWest returns the £100 million with interest. But what would happen if NatWest were to become bankrupt? Of course, the insolvency of a major high-street British bank is very unlikely; but it is not impossible. In this unlikely event, HSBC would lose its £100 million.

This insolvency risk, also known as credit risk or default risk, is very important. Banks deal not only with each other, and not only with top-quality financial institutions from countries with honest and competent financial supervision, but also with riskier entities (people, companies, or even governments). With some of these entities the risk of insolvency is significant.

The solution is called *repo*. Just as before, the bank lends its client the money. Also, the client lends the bank government bonds (described in Chapter 2) of the same value and over the same period of time. If the bank were lending £100 million cash for 3 months to a client, the client would lend £100 million worth of government bonds for the same period of time. The loan is said to be *collateralised*, and the government bonds are the *collateral*.

Under normal circumstances, after 3 months the client returns the £100 million plus interest, and the bank returns the bonds. But if the client should become insolvent and be unable to pay the money, the bank can recover its loss by selling the collateral that it holds.

For the bank that is lending money, the advantage of collateralisation is that it almost eliminates the credit risk. For the borrower of money, the disadvantage is that collateral must be found. The borrower's disadvantage and the lender's advantage are reflected in the price; the interest rate on a collateralised loan is below that on a non-collateralised loan. The precise gap varies across currencies, and within a currency it varies across maturities and according to the quality of the collateral and the counterparty, but a typical unsecured–secured differential is 0.1% to 0.5%.

It might help the reader to liken a repo to a residential mortgage. In both cases the cost of borrowing is cheapened by giving collateral to the lender. In one case the collateral is a financial asset, in the other the legal rights to a property. Of course, a mortgage can only be used to borrow money if one has a property, or is going to use the money to buy a property. Likewise, repo can only be used to cheapen the cost of borrowing for those who own suitable collateral, or who are going to use the money to buy that collateral.

In this example the collateral used was a government bond. By turnover and volume outstanding, this is the most common form of repo. But the parties may well agree to use other collateral, and there is a repo market in corporate bonds and other financial assets.

The origin of the term 'repo' is a contraction of the word 'repurchase'. In a repurchase agreement, a borrower of money would sell some financial asset to the lender of money, and at the same time agree to a later repurchase of that asset. The effect was that of a collateralised loan, with the interest rate being a function of the ratio of the sale and repurchase prices. This sale and repurchase is no longer the usual way to trade repo; the modern repo legal agreement more robustly manages a default by either side.

So in summary a repo is just a collateralised deposit. The collateral increases the creditworthiness and hence reduces the interest rate on the deposit.

Central-bank money-market operations

The news services give the impression that central banks decide interest rates. For example, they might report that the Federal Reserve raised the interest rate from 6% to 6.50%, or that the European Central Bank raised rates by a quarter percent to 4.25%, or that the Bank of England left rates unchanged at 6%.

But we have just seen that banks lend money to each other at rates chosen by the market. There is no seeking of permission from a central bank: if Goldman Sachs is willing to lend 1-month US dollars at 6.2%, and CSFB is willing to borrow, then they trade. So what does the official interest rate mean, and how do central banks implement it?

Recall that many commercial banks have accounts with the central bank. These accounts are subject to rules about overdrafts, each central bank having its own rules. Some central banks prohibit overdrafts; at the end of each day no account may be overdrawn. Other central banks are less strict, specifying that every account must have a positive balance on average, where the averaging is conducted over a period of time known as a *reserve period*.

Whichever the case, commercial banks need to avoid having an overdraft at the central bank, either on average or every day. So what can an overdrawn bank do? It can borrow money from another bank. But this only works if, between them, the banks have enough. If their balances total an overdrawn state, then borrowing money from each other only passes the overdraft around. Bank-to-bank borrowing can only move rather than extinguish the overdraft. The escape is to borrow money directly from the central bank. And the rate at which the central bank lends money can indeed be chosen by the central bank; this is the rate that makes the headlines.

In their money-market operations, almost all central banks lend money against collateral; they use repo rather than accept the credit risk of unsecured lending. For some the only eligible collateral in this repo operation is the debt of the local government; others accept almost anything. The remaining details of the intervention also vary considerably from central bank to central bank: some intervene every day, others once a week; some lend money overnight, others for weeks at a time.

Some central banks occasionally use a form of auction to choose the rate at which funds are lent to the market. This is known as a *floating* or *variable* policy rate, but even when this is used the central bank sometimes determines the outcome in advance by specifying that bids below a certain cutoff will not be accepted. Whatever the detail of the central bank's money-market operations, the commercial banks are obliged to turn to the central bank to clear their overdrafts. Thus central banks have great control over short-term interest rates.

Two money markets

One might expect that a currency's money market would be based in that currency's financial capital: US dollars in New York, sterling in London, yen in Tokyo, Swiss francs in Zurich, etc. This was so until the late 1950s, when the Soviet Union, concerned that its dollar deposits in New York might be frozen by the US government, opened a dollar account with a European bank. Then in 1963 the US introduced Regulation Q, which imposed a maximum rate of interest that could be paid on domestic dollar deposits, and in 1965 introduced a lending tax.

The upshot of this regulation was that banks benefited from doing business outside the reach of US law, and London came to dominate this offshore dollar business. Accounts 'in London' are subject to the law of England and Wales, so US sanctions, restrictions and taxes cannot apply. In time the banks in London, often branches of US banks, started actively trading deposits in other currencies as well.

Nowadays regulation is lighter, and so money can be moved cheaply to and from London; therefore the price of London money generally tracks very closely that of domestic money. But there have been differences between domestic and London interest rates. These differences have had different causes at different times: tax laws, bank regulations, the possibility that a country might introduce exchange controls, and the differences between the creditworthiness of the banks in London and those in the domestic market.

The London money market is particularly active in dollars, sterling, euros, yen, and Swiss francs, with less liquidity (ease of trading in large size) in Australian, Canadian and New Zealand dollars. Deposits in most other currencies trade only in their domestic market.

The terminology for London money is confusing. When dollar deposits started to trade in London, they were called *eurodollars*, the 'euro' prefix then meaning that the currency was outside its home jurisdiction. And hence *euromarks* for London-traded Deutschmarks, *eurolira* for Italian lira in London, *euroyen*, *euroswiss*, and so on. The use of the 'euro' terminology subsequently became more widespread. Much corporate debt (discussed in more detail later) is issued under the law of England and Wales, even if the currency is that of the US, Germany or Switzerland. Thus tradable debt (bonds) issued in London became known as *eurobonds*.

Now fast-forward to 1999, the start of Europe's single currency, called the euro. The words 'eurodollar' and 'euroswiss' become ambiguous. They still refer to London-delivery dollars and Swiss, but now they can also mean exchange rates between euros and US

11

dollars and between euros and Swiss francs. On rare occasions one even hears the term 'euroeuro' for London-delivery euros. So the word 'euro' needs to be interpreted with care.

The euro

Several European countries, including Germany, the Netherlands, France, Italy and Spain, are members of EMU, Europe's Economic and Monetary Union. These countries share a common currency called the euro, their former national currencies having been merged together. This irrevocable merger was achieved by legal diktat, and now, in law, each of the former national currencies is a denomination of the euro.

There are 100 cents in the US dollar. US law is clear: if you are owed 100¢, then you are owed $1. This 100-to-1 'exchange rate' is irrevocable; it cannot be changed. Indeed, if you deposit in your bank account 1000¢, and then deposit $10, the bank does not keep a separate tally of how many dollars and how many cents have been deposited, it only knows that the account contains $20.

Under European law, and the law of the countries of the EU, the euro is no different. It too comes in various denominations, including the euro cent (at an exchange rate of 100 to 1), the Deutschmark (at an exchange rate of 1.95583 to 1), the Dutch guilder (2.20371 to 1), the French franc (6.55957 to 1), etc. Legally, the Deutschmark exists as a currency in the same sense that the US cent exists: the Deutschmark is a denomination of a primary currency, the euro, albeit a non-decimal denomination.

Note that US dollars and US cents have different physical manifestations, the former on paper printed green on white, the latter as metal coins. This makes no difference; they are still the same currency. Likewise, the Deutschmark and the French franc have different physical forms—but this too is irrelevant, because they are both denominations of the euro.

Banks quote the same interest rate for deposits in dollars and deposits in cents, because they are the same currency. Likewise, it must be the same interest rate for deposits in euros, Deutschmarks, Dutch guilders, French francs and the former national currencies of the other EMU members, because they are all the same currency. And because these are all the same currency, wholesale financial markets quote prices in euro, not in the former national currencies.

Writing money

Having discussed the ambiguities in the word 'euro', it is worth mentioning other possible sources of ambiguity in the writing of money. One might think that '$100m' means one hundred million dollars. But the 'm' is ambiguous. In English 'm' means a million, in French it is the abbreviation for 'mille', meaning a thousand (though the abbreviation is more usually written in uppercase). A French speaker would write one hundred million as 100MM, and could well read 100m as one hundred thousand. And the dollars are ambiguous; they could be from any one of a number of countries, including the US, Canada, Australia, New Zealand and Singapore.

To avoid ambiguity in currency names, international standard ISO 4217 specifies official currency abbreviations. Each of these abbreviations has 3 letters: in most cases the first two letters identify the country, the third the currency. Codes for the most important currencies are shown in the table overleaf. Henceforth it will be assumed that readers are comfortable with the first seven in this list: USD, EUR, JPY, GBP, CHF, CAD and AUD, and at least approximately with their current values.

Money amounts should be written unambiguously: USD 100 million and USD 100,000,000 are both clear. Unless the context is clear and not legally binding, readers are advised to avoid use of the suffix 'm'.

The word 'billion' used to be ambiguous. In American English a billion is a thousand million; in old British English it used to mean a million million and it still does in some other languages. But in English the Americans have won: a billion is always a

Code	Currency
USD	US dollar
EUR	Euro
JPY	Japanese yen
GBP	UK pound (sterling)
CHF	Swiss franc
CAD	Canadian dollar
AUD	Australian dollar
NZD	New Zealand dollar
MXN	Mexican (new) peso
SEK	Swedish krone
DKK	Danish krone
NOK	Norwegian krone
PLN	Polish (new) zloty
HUF	Hungarian forint
CZK	Czech krone
ZAR	South African rand
SGD	Singapore dollar
RUB	Russian, new rouble

Former national currencies now absorbed into the euro

DEM	German mark
NLG	Dutch guilder, florin
FRF	French franc
ITL	Italian lira
ESP	Spanish peseta

Codes beginning with X have special meanings

XEU	ECU, now the euro
XAU	Gold
XAG	Silver
XPT	Platinum
XPD	Palladium

thousand million, and a trillion is always a million million. Because the words 'million' and 'billion' sound so similar, in spoken English the word 'yard' (a contraction of 'milliard') is often used as a synonym for a thousand million.

Care should also be taken when writing and reading dates. In America '03/10/08' is March 10, 2008; in most of the rest of the world it is 03 October 2008.

Settlement details

There is a detail about money markets that will prove important later. In most currencies the money market is said to be 'T+2'. This means that settlement, when delivery of funds takes place, occurs 2 business days after the *trade date* (the 'T' in 'T+2'). The *settlement date* is also known as the *value date*.

So if on Monday 13 August 2007 J. P. Morgan agrees to lend USD to CSFB for 3 months, J. P. Morgan would pay this money to CSFB two days after trading, on 15 August, and it would be returned with interest 3 months after that, on 15 November 2007. Most currencies' money markets are T+2, including USD, EUR, JPY and CHF. The main exception to T+2 is sterling, which is T+0, also known as *same-day settlement*. In sterling, standard practice is to settle a trade on the same day that it is agreed. However, counterparties can always agree to a non-standard settlement, but in the absence of such agreement, GBP is T+0 and almost all others are T+2.

The trading timetable for deposits

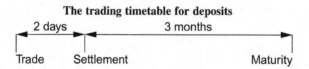

There is a standard definition of the seemingly simple phrase '3 months'. For example, when is 3 months after 30 November 2009? It can't be 30 February 2010, because there isn't such a day. And it can't even be 28 February 2010, because that is a Sunday. As it is, the official definition from the International Swap Dealers Association (ISDA) says that 3 months after Monday 30 November 2009 is Friday 26 February 2010, but the point is that there is a precise definition.

Summary

- Payments in the real economy cause banks' balances with the central bank to rise and fall. A bank with a shortfall will want to borrow it from a bank with an excess, and hence there is an interbank deposit market (a money market).
- This market exists, with maturities from 1 day to 1 year, in every currency, and in the major currencies it exists both domestically and in London.
- A market participant, by choosing to borrow or lend money at any particular maturity, is implicitly speculating against the forward rates implied by the spot rates.
- Banks also lend money against collateral; the secured nature of this lending reduces the credit risk, and hence it reduces the interest rate.
- Central banks have great control over short-term interest rates.
- The euro is a legal construct that makes the former national currency units irrelevant to wholesale financial markets.

Chapter 2

Government bonds

Introduction

The oldest wholesale financial market is in government debt. Governments have always found it more difficult to tax than to spend—on the pleasures of the court, fighting wars, welfare, or even just repaying the previous borrowing. So governments borrow money, and they have found that the cheapest way to do this is to issue tradable government debt.

Let us move to an example. At the start of 2000, the German government auctioned a new bond, the euro-denominated 6.25% of 04 January 2030. Owners of €100 *nominal*, also called *face value* or *notional*, of this bond receive a *coupon* of €6.25 on every 04 January until and including 04 January 2030, when holders also receive the *principal* of €100.

Note that the payments to a holder are defined per nominal. To repeat: €100 nominal of this bond pays a coupon of €6.25 every 04 January, and also a principal of €100 at maturity. That does not mean the market price of this bundle of payments is €100. If the market deems 6.25% to be a generous coupon, this bond will cost more than €100. And if the market deems 6.25% to be miserly, the bond will cost less. The nominal amount simply defines the payments.

In January 2000 the German government sold €5 billion nominal of this bond by auction. The market thought that 6.25% was slightly generous, so was willing to pay slightly more than €100 per €100 nominal: the auction price was slightly over *par*, i.e. slightly over 100. In this manner the German government borrowed just over €5.02 billion from the financial markets, money which it could then spend immediately.

It may be helpful to imagine a bearer bond, that is, a bond in paper form rather than electronic form. A bearer bond is marked with the face value in large type, say 100, in some particular currency. Coupons are attached down the side, and these are marked with their value, here 6.25, and their payment date. On a coupon day the holder presents the bond to the issuer or its agent, the appropriate coupon is cut off (the word 'coupon' being derived from the French verb *couper* 'to cut') and 6.25 paid to the holder. So for any particular face value the size of the payments is fixed—it's printed on the bond certificate. However, although the payments are fixed, the bond itself might have a market price above or below the face value, and this market price can fluctuate.

The concept of yield

So, a government bond pays a series of cashflows, in the form of interest coupons and a final principal. The sizes of these payments are known in advance. A bond is just a tradable promise to pay a bundle of future cashflows. These tradable bundles are almost synonymously known as *bonds*, *securities*, *notes*, *paper* and *debt*.

For ease of analysis, let us start by considering the simplest type of tradable government debt. Many governments sell a particular type of short-term debt that pays a single cashflow of 100 at maturity—only the principal is paid, no coupons. This type of debt is called a *Treasury bill*, usually abbreviated to *T-bill*.

So let us consider a T-bill that matures in 1 year. If this costs 100 then the purchaser in effect receives no interest (lends 100 now, repaid 100 at maturity, implies an interest rate of 0%). If this 1-year T-bill costs 99 (lends 99 now, repaid 100 at maturity), the purchaser is in effect being paid an interest rate of about 1%. And if it costs 95, the purchaser is in effect being paid an interest rate of a little over 5%. This effective interest rate is called the *yield*. Observe that a lower price means a higher yield, and a higher price means a lower yield. This is crucial:

- Price up = yield down
- Price down = yield up

Example yield calculations

We now emphasise this rule with a series of examples. In each example let us consider a coupon-paying bond with a nominal coupon of 6%, so the interest payments are 6 currency units per year. For example, a 3-year bond with an annual coupon of 6% pays 6 currency units at the end of year 1, the same again at the end of year 2, and 106 when it matures at the end of year 3. This stream of cashflows is fixed when the bond is created, and does not depend on the price of the bond. Whether the bond costs 90 or 110, the size and timing of these cashflows are fixed, which is why bonds are known as *fixed-income* investments.

Let us consider a 1-year bond paying this coupon of 6%. We are therefore considering a bond that has a single payment of 106 at the end of year 1. If a bond that pays 106 in 1 year costs 100, then the purchaser is receiving an effective interest rate (a yield) of 6%. This relationship can be turned round: if this cashflow (106 in 1 year) costs a price that implies a yield of 6%, then that price must be 100. Therefore, for a bond with this cashflow (106 in 1 year), saying that it costs 100 is equivalent to saying that it yields 6%. More generally, for any given bond, for any set of known fixed cashflows, a price implies a yield and a yield implies a price.

PRICING MONEY

At what price would this 1-year 6% bond yield 5%? If the yield is 5% then 100 currency units today are worth the same as 105 units in 1 year:

$$100 \text{ today} = 105 \text{ in 1 year}$$

Dividing by 100 gives that

$$1 \text{ today} = 1.05 \text{ in 1 year}$$

dividing by 1.05 gives that

$$1 \div 1.05 \text{ today} = 1 \text{ in 1 year}$$

and multiplying by 106, we conclude that

$$106 \div 1.05 \text{ today} = 106 \text{ in 1 year}$$

Thus, at a 5% yield, 106 in 1 year (which is what the bond pays) is worth $106 \div 1.05 \approx 100.95$ today. And hence saying that this bond costs 100.95 is equivalent to saying that it yields 5%. Note again that a higher price is equivalent to a lower yield. And if the same bond is priced to yield 7%, then it must cost $106 \div 1.07 \approx 99.07$. Again, yield up implies price down.

What about a 2-year bond? Well, 100 nominal of a 2-year bond with a 6% annual coupon pays 6 currency units after 1 year and 106 after 2 years. Clearly, if the yield is 5% then

$$6 \div 1.05 \text{ today} = 6 \text{ in 1 year}$$

So the first payment on the two-year bond is 6, and today that is worth $6 \div 1.05$. What about the second payment? We know that

$$1 \text{ today} = 1.05 \text{ in 1 year}$$

and likewise that

$$1 \text{ in 1 year} = 1.05 \text{ in 2 years}$$

so

$$1 \text{ today} = 1.05 \times 1.05 \text{ in 2 years}$$

This is just compound interest; assuming a 5% yield, 1 unit today is worth the same as 1.05 in a year is worth the same as $1.05^2 = 1.1025$ in 2 years.

Thus the second payment, of 106 in 2 years' time, is worth
$106 \div 1.1025$. The two payments together are therefore worth
$(6 \div 1.05) + (106 \div 1.05^2) \approx 101.86$.

Observe that a 6% 1-year bond and a 6% 2-year bond each cost
exactly 100 when yielding 6%. And that the yield falling to 5% is
equivalent to the price increasing by 0.95 for the 1-year bond, but
increasing by 1.86 for the 2-year bond. This illustrates a general
rule: longer bonds are more sensitive to changes in yield. So for
any given change in interest rates, a longer bond's price will
change by more than a shorter bond's price.

Prices of bonds with a 6% nominal coupon

Maturity (years)	Yield				
	4%	5%	6%	7%	8%
1	101.92	100.95	100.00	99.07	98.15
2	103.77	101.86	100.00	98.19	96.43
5	108.90	104.33	100.00	95.90	92.01
10	116.22	107.72	100.00	92.98	86.58
30	134.58	115.37	100.00	87.59	77.48

The effect of this rule can be seen in the table and the chart
overleaf, which show the prices of 6% bonds of various maturities
at various different yields. Observe that a higher yield means a
lower price, and that the longer-dated securities move further in
price for any given change in yield.

Price–yield relationships for bonds of various maturities

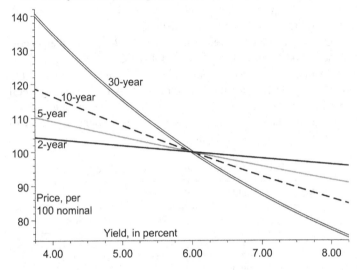

Coupon and yield

Once again, let us restate the difference between coupon and yield:

- The coupon of a bond defines the payments made. The coupon is known when the bond is first issued, and remains constant until maturity. The bond's coupon is not altered by a change in the bond's price.
- The yield is the effective interest rate, calculated from the price of the bond. The market determines the price, and hence the yield. As time passes, or as the price changes, the yield also changes.

In other words, coupon is the interest rate paid per 100 nominal of the bond; yield is the effective interest rate paid per 100 cost.

The yield curve

In Chapter 1 we saw that deposits of different maturities have different interest rates. The same is true of government bonds: different government bonds have different yields. The prices of deposits of different terms are driven by the prospects for the path of interest rates in the future, and exactly the same principle applies to government bonds. If the market believes that interest rates are rising over the long term, longer-dated bonds will yield more than shorter-dated bonds. In this case the *yield curve* would be described as *positive*, or upward-sloping.

The following chart shows yields of various bonds issued by the government of the Australian Commonwealth, as of 21 January 2000. Maturity is plotted on the *x*-axis and yield on the *y*-axis. Bonds of different maturities have different yields.

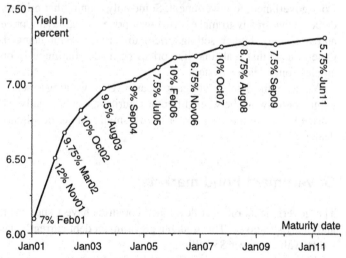

Yields of Australian Commonwealth government bonds as of 21 January 2000

The steepness of the yield curve is usually quoted in hundredths of a percent, called *basis points* and abbreviated to 'bp'. So '2s10s are +16bp', read as 'twos-tens are plus sixteen', means that the government bond with 10 years to maturity (or the one nearest to 10 years) yields 0.16% more than the government bond with 2 years to maturity (or the one nearest to 2 years). The steepness of the yield curve is actively traded; this is discussed in Chapter 12.

Primary dealers

Most governments appoint dealers in their bonds. Bonds are sold at auction, and typically only these *primary dealers* are allowed to bid. In return for this privilege, the primary dealers are obliged to make markets in that government's debt; dealers must quote prices to clients.

This is an obligation; dealers must make markets in conditions fair and foul. However, the precise nature of this obligation varies from government to government. Some only require that primary dealers stand ready to make a two-way price (i.e. a buying price and a slightly higher selling price) to customers on demand. Others insist that real-time live prices be made continuously on an electronic dealing system.

Whatever the detailed obligations, an investor wanting to sell or to buy, or to switch between different securities, would usually ask a price from a primary dealer, or from a small number of primary dealers.

Government bond markets

The governments of most developed countries have issued debt, and many still do so. This tradable government debt currently has a total value of over $5 trillion.

US government bonds are issued by the Treasury Department and are called Treasuries. As of late 2000 the total value of outstanding Treasuries was almost \$1.9 trillion. US Treasuries (USTs) pay coupons semi-annually, so \$100 nominal of the 8% Treasury of 15 Nov 2021 pays coupons of \$4 every 15 May and 15 November. US government securities with an initial maturity of 10 years or less are called *Notes*, those with an initial maturity of more than 10 years are called *Bonds*; both are known as Treasuries or USTs. The prices of USTs are quoted in thirty-secondths rather than in decimal, and hence a price of 98-28 means $98\frac{28}{32} = 98.875$. A '+' indicates half a $\frac{1}{32}$, so 99-24+ is $99 + \frac{24}{32} + \frac{1}{64} = 99.765625$. The US is the only country still quoting the price of its debt in these fractions.

British government debt used to be issued in the form of paper securities that had a gilt edge, and they are still called *gilt-edged securities*, or *gilts* for short. Gilts date back to the founding of the Bank of England in 1694, and like USTs have semi-annual coupons. Outstanding gilts total about £300 billion.

All the large eurozone governments have issued fixed-coupon bonds. Those of Germany and France total about €600 billion and €500 billion respectively, and they pay annual coupons. As in the US, the name of the debt depends on the initial maturity. German paper is issued with one of 2, 5, 10 or 30 years to maturity. The 2-year paper is called Schätze (a contraction of a much longer German noun), the 5-year OBL, and the 10- and 30-year Bund. French government debt with 5 years or less at issue is called BTAN; debt with longer than 5 years at first issue is called OAT. The short names quoted here are used fluently by participants in these markets, but they do not affect the cash-flows or the creditworthiness of the issuer. Tradable Italian government debt totals about €1 trillion, and exists in a number of different forms, the largest and most important of which is the fixed-coupon BTP.

The Japanese government bond (JGB) market has in recent years become huge (some ¥370 trillion), and is still growing at tens of trillions of yen per annum. It pays coupons semi-annually.

Repo as part of the government-bond market

Repo was discussed in Chapter 1. When borrowing money, repo can be used to improve the credit quality of a loan and so reduce the interest rate. The cost of secured borrowing is typically about 10bp to 50bp less than that of unsecured borrowing, though the differential varies from currency to currency, from maturity to maturity, and over time.

But repo is not only a money-market instrument; it is also a bond-market instrument. Consider the position of a bond dealer who has sold a bond to an investor. If the dealer already owned that bond, then delivery is easy and the sale lightens the dealer's inventory. But what if the dealer didn't own the bond? To be able to deliver the bond to the investor, the dealer must borrow that bond. The dealer would borrow the bond from a third party, and lend money to that third party. This is a repo, and the interest rate paid on this cash deposit is the price of the repo.

In a typical government bond market, most bonds will not be in particular demand and will trade at the same repo rate. This rate is often called *general collateral* (GC). But if many market participants are trying to borrow a particular bond, the demand for that bond will be reflected in the price: the interest rate paid on the deposit will be low. A bond that is more in demand will have a lower repo rate and is said to be *tight* or *special*.

If a bond is special, a dealer can use that bond as collateral to borrow money cheaply, by lending the bond and borrowing money at a sub-GC rate. That access to cheap funding is a perk of owning the bond, and means this bond will tend to trade expensively relative to other non-special bonds of similar maturity. Hence there is a close relationship between repo and the relative cheapness or expensiveness of different government bonds.

Accrued interest

It used to be that a bond cost the price that was quoted. If the quoted price was 102, the cost of the bond was 102, per 100 nominal, in the appropriate currency. This was a clear and easy way to do things. However, it did mean that bonds appeared to collapse in price when a coupon was paid. If a bond paid a coupon of 3 currency units, the quoted price would typically drop by about 3, as the coupon just paid fell out of the price. So the way that prices are quoted was changed.

Prices are now quoted *clean*, that is without accrued interest. If a bond is halfway through its coupon period, and the next coupon is to be 3, then the buyer pays 1.50 more than the quoted clean price. If the bond is two-thirds through its coupon period, the accrued interest is 2. If the bond is almost at the end of its coupon period, the accrued interest is almost 3; when the coupon is paid, the fall in the accrued interest (from just under 3 to zero) offsets the change in value. A bond's *value* is its *dirty price*, which equals its clean price plus its accrued interest; this is also known as its *present value* or its *cost*.

This *accrued interest* can be thought of as reimbursement for the seller. If the seller has sold the bond two-thirds of the way through the coupon period, then the seller is, in some sense, entitled to two-thirds of the coupon. In some jurisdictions this entitlement to a proportion of the coupon, as reflected in the payment of accrued interest, has taxation consequences. However, bond trading is now much less tax-dependent than it was.

Note though that *equities*, known as *shares* in the UK and *stocks* in the US, are still quoted dirty; the equity price drops as a coupon is paid. Also, in the equity markets, a coupon is usually called a *dividend* and is not of fixed size.

STRIPS

A US government bond pays coupons every half-year until maturity, when the principal of $100 is also paid. But what if, for some particular need, an investor wishes to acquire a different shape of cashflows? For example, what if an investor wishes to put money away until 2021 and not receive any coupons before then? Or what if that investor wishes to receive coupons, and only coupons, from 2016 until 2021?

Because there is sometimes a demand for such customised collections of cashflows, the US government allows bonds to be *stripped*. This is an exchange facility; a dealer hands in a US Treasury and receives in return the same cashflows but in separately tradable form. These cashflows are called STRIPS, short for Separately Traded Registered Interest and Principal Securities.

Stripping breaks a bond into its individual cashflows. Stripping a bond exchanges it for its *principal strip*, also called its *principal only* (PO), and its *coupon strips*, also called interest strips or *interest onlys* (IOs). If the date is now summer 2002, stripping $100 million nominal of the US Treasury 8% Nov 2021 produces $4 million nominal of the Nov 2002 coupon strip, $4 million nominal of the May 2003 coupon strip, and the same amount of each coupon strip until 15 Nov 2021, as well $100 million nominal of the principal strip, dated 15 Nov 2021. Stripping the bond has therefore exchanged one bundle of cashflows (joined together in a single bond) for a bundle of the same cashflows (but in a separately tradable form).

Equally, it is possible to *reconstitute* a bond from its strips. If one hands over the principal strip and the correct amounts of the coupon strips, one receives the original bond in return.

There is a technical difference between coupon strips and principal strips. Principal strips come from a particular bond. One cannot reconstitute a bond using a same-maturity coupon strip instead of the principal strip, or by using a same-maturity principal strip from a different bond. In other words, the principal strips are marked with the name of the source bond; in order to reconstitute a bond, one needs a principal strip from that same bond.

But coupon strips are not marked with their source. Consider stripping the 8% Nov 2021 and selling some of the Nov 2005 strip. Later one could strip the May 2006 Treasury and use the resulting

Nov 2005 coupon strip as part of the reconstitution of the 8% Nov 2021.

Several governments have a stripping facility. Almost all US Treasuries are strippable, but in practice the only USTs that are stripped are those that pay coupons on either 15 February and August or 15 May and November. France also has a strip market, though it is not as heavily traded as in the US. The UK strip market is less active than the French strip market, and there is even less activity in stripping German Bunds, Italian BTPs, Spanish Bonos, Dutch State Loans and Belgian OLOs.

A strip pays a single cashflow at maturity, and no intervening coupons. Bonds with this property are known as *zero-coupon bonds*. Because strips are zero-coupon, there is no accrued interest. For this reason, in some jurisdictions they are taxed differently to ordinary coupon-paying bonds.

Other tradable government debt

All the examples above referred to government debt with fixed cashflows. Governments also issue other types of debt. Inflation-linked debt has cashflows that increase in line with retail consumer prices. The details differ from country to country, but the broad principle is the same. The payments made by the issuer to the holder are specified in *real terms*, that is, in money with constant purchasing power.

For example, inflation-linked British government bonds are called index-linked gilts (ILGs) and are described by the UK Debt Management Office as

> gilts on which both the [coupons] and the capital repayment on redemption are adjusted in line with inflation (as measured by the Retail Prices Index, or RPI). Investors are thus protected against the value of their investments being eroded by inflation.

So let us consider the last three cashflows of the $2\frac{1}{2}$% inflation-linked gilt that matured on 24 September 2001. If this had been a conventional gilt, then the final two semi-annual coupons, paid in March and September 2001, would each have been £1.25, and the principal (paid on the same day as the final coupon) would have been £100. But the payments of an ILG are indexed to retail prices, which had more than doubled since the bond was first issued: the penultimate coupon was £2.7227, the final coupon was £2.7323 and the principal was £218.5846.

Conceptually it is useful to think of such a bond as being denominated in bread and beer, or some other real tangible thing, rather than in monetary units. Imagine buying a bond for 100 units of real goods, and that this bond pays the holder 3 units of these goods every year until maturity, when it pays 100 units. This investment would return 3% more than inflation. But to avoid the inconvenience of physically delivering a basket of goods, inflation-linked bonds pay the equivalent of this basket in cash. The payments on an inflation-linked bond are therefore real rather than nominal, and its yield is also quoted real. And hence a quoted yield of 3% means that the holder is in effect paid inflation plus 3%.

Various countries have issued inflation-linked debt: index-linked gilts by the UK since 1981; Real-Return Bonds (RRBs) by Canada since 1991; and Treasury Inflation-Protected Securities (TIPS) by the US since 1997. Australia, Sweden and France have also issued inflation-linked securities.

Some governments have issued floating-rate debt. Floating-rate notes (FRNs) pay a coupon that varies with short-term interbank interest rates. At the start of each coupon period, the level of interbank interest rates is noted. This level is the *Libor fixing* (defined in Chapter 3) and it is used to calculate the coupon that is paid at the end of the period. Buying an FRN at 100 is therefore much like leaving the money on deposit at the bank at a floating rate. Of course, if the FRN is issued by the government, the credit is superior to that of a commercial bank, a fact reflected in the price. Very little floating-rate government debt is issued nowadays, but other entities, especially financial institutions, issue large quantities of FRNs.

Non-government debt

So we have examined government debt and hinted at the existence of non-government debt. Actually, there is as much non-government tradable debt as government tradable debt. Indeed, for a small number of large investment banks, the issuance of non-government debt is a highly profitable business.

The key difference between government debt and non-government debt is the possibility of default. If a government is borrowing money in a currency over which it is sovereign, it can always print money to pay the bondholders. But if the money is being borrowed by a commercial bank or an industrial corporation, or even by a government issuing in a foreign currency, the bondholder cannot be sure of being paid. A bondholder will require compensation for this risk of default, so the yield of a non-government bond will typically be higher than the yield of a government bond with similar cashflows.

The boundary between government and non-government debt is not entirely clear-cut. The governments of the eurozone are not individually sovereign over the euro, so any one of them could default (assuming that it was not rescued by the others). Indeed, when the UK has borrowed in euros, it has done so more cheaply than Italy, despite the fact that Italy is a eurozone government and the UK is not. Furthermore, the US, Japan and various European countries each have borrowers that are widely assumed to be guaranteed by the government, despite the absence of a formal written guarantee.

Whoever the issuer, a lender will typically want a higher return than on a domestic government bond with similar cashflows. How much higher depends primarily on the creditworthiness of the issuer, and when assessing the creditworthiness of a particular issuer, a buyer of debt will be strongly guided by the opinion of a *rating agency*.

Rating agencies

Rating agencies publish their opinion of the creditworthiness of many borrowers and bonds. These opinions are known as credit ratings. The three most prominent rating agencies are Moody's, Standard & Poor's and Fitch. The table shows the long-term investment-grade senior ratings. For each agency the top rating is known as triple-A, with each of the lower ratings coming in three subcategories. Below the investment-grade ratings listed in the table come the speculative ratings of double-B and single-B, then the near-default C ratings and finally the in-default D ratings.

As a guide, a small number of government issuers are triple-A, including those of Switzerland, UK, US, Norway, Netherlands, Germany, France, Austria, and some minnows such as Liechtenstein. Also triple-A are most of the large supranational borrowers, including the International Bank for Reconstruction and Development (IBRD), more commonly known as the World Bank, the European Investment Bank (EIB) and the European Bank for Reconstruction and Development (EBRD). Triple-A borrowers can generally access funds at a rate cheaper than 1% to 2% over the local government.

Moody's	S&P	Fitch	Meaning
Aaa	AAA	AAA	Triple-A: highest quality
Aa1	Aa1	AA+	Double-A: very high credit quality, very strong
Aa2	AA	AA	capacity for timely payment, not significantly
Aa3	AA–	AA–	vulnerable to foreseeable events
A1	A+	A+	Single-A: high credit quality, strong capacity
A2	A	A	for timely payment, more vulnerable to
A3	A–	A–	changes in circumstances
Baa1	BBB+	BBB+	Triple-B: good credit quality, adequate
Baa2	BBB	BBB	capacity for timely payment, but adverse
Baa3	BBB–	BBB–	changes in circumstances more likely to impair

Banks and other private sector financial institutions are typically double-A; a bank whose rating falls much below this will have difficulty borrowing money on economic terms in the interbank money market. Industrial companies span the whole range of ratings. Changes in ratings often cause changes in price, and hence many analysts are employed to predict these changes.

Summary

- Governments borrow money, mostly by selling fixed-coupon bonds.
- Price up = yield down; price down = yield up.
- For any given change in yield, longer bonds change in price by more than shorter bonds.
- Dealers borrow bonds using repo.
- A dealer buying a bond may well borrow the money to do so, cheapening that borrowing using repo.
- Some government bonds are strippable; they can be exchanged for the same bundle of cashflows in separately tradable form.
- Entities other than governments also issue bonds, and the additional yield over the debt of the government is dependent on the credit rating.

Chapter 3

Futures

The gold miner's problem

Consider the position of an entrepreneur about to open a gold mine. This entrepreneur knows that gold can be extracted from the ground and purified for less than, say, $250 per troy ounce, including all costs. Gold is now trading at $275/oz, but it will take a while for the mine to be built and extraction to start. The problem is that the entrepreneur cannot know whether the price of gold will still be above $250/oz when it is available for sale.

So our entrepreneur wants to sell gold for delivery in 1 year, at a price agreed now. A dealer is asked to *bid* (to state a buying price) for gold, not for immediate (spot) delivery but for *forward* delivery in 1 year. A price is made: let us say that the dealer bids $280/oz. Recall from Chapter 1 that the forward price is not necessarily the same as the spot price.

But our entrepreneur is not yet in the clear. What if the price of gold collapses and the dealer goes bankrupt? The bankruptcy means that the contract, to sell a certain quantity of gold at $280/oz, is worthless. Instead the entrepreneur must take the low market price then prevailing. So this expert in gold mining must now become an expert in assessing credit risk.

It gets worse. Let us imagine that the agreed forward delivery was for any date in June. But later the miner realises that production is running two months behind schedule. The miner would now need to buy back the June-delivery gold that had previously been sold, and instead sell August-delivery gold. If the miner had sold June-delivery gold to a particular dealer, and later repurchased June-delivery gold from a different dealer, then the two contracts would not fully offset—there would be credit exposure to both dealers.

The gold miner's solution

There is a better way, known as a futures contract. An exchange allows a number of futures contracts to be traded. Each contract is a contract to buy or deliver an asset at some time in the future. For example, COMEX, a division of the New York Mercantile Exchange, trades a contract against which 100 troy ounces of gold are delivered.

For every futures contract, there is a central counterparty; the buyer and seller each have a contract with that central counterparty, not with each other. The central counterparty is known as a *clearing house*, and the creditworthiness of a clearing house is always excellent. If the miner sells and the speculator buys, the legal position is that each has traded with the clearing house. And if the miner were to sell and later to buy, the two contracts (both with the clearing house) would cancel out. All that would remain would be the profit or loss from the difference between the buying and selling prices. And hence both buyer and seller are exposed only to the credit of the clearing house.

The futures contracts are standardised, which eliminates costs of negotiation. A gold futures contract specifies in detail the minimum purity of the gold, where it must be delivered, its form, and every other relevant detail.

Futures contracts are traded on many different *underlying* assets. There are contracts on gold and platinum, on various kinds of wheat, on pig bellies and orange juice, on various grades of oil, on government debt, on equity indices such as the S&P 500 and the FTSE 100, and even on interbank interest rates. Each of these contracts specifies in detail what must be delivered at expiry: how much of what quality to where.

The value of a futures contract derives from the value of the underlying asset. For this reason, futures contracts, and many other types of tradable contracts, are known as *derivatives*.

Contract specification

As an example, the following extract has been taken from the specification of the COMEX gold contract:

> In fulfilment of each contract, the seller must deliver 100 troy ounces ... of refined gold, assaying not less than .995 fineness, cast either in one bar or in three ... bars, and bearing a serial number and identifying stamp of a refiner approved and listed by the Exchange. ...
>
> Delivery must be made from a depository located in the Borough of Manhattan, New York City, licensed by the Exchange. ...
>
> The first delivery day is the first business day of the delivery month; the last delivery day is the last business day of the delivery month.

The twenty-six approved refiners range from the Sheffield Smelting Co. Ltd of Sheffield, England, to the Union of Soviet Socialist Republics (which, it's true, has disappeared, but there are still ingots bearing its hammer-and-sickle stamp). The three approved depositories are Morgan Guaranty Trust Company of New York, the Republic National Bank of New York and the Scotia Mocatta Depository Corporation.

The object is not to tire the reader with the detailed specification for this particular contract, but rather to emphasise that every futures contract has a detailed specification. Buyers and sellers alike know exactly what can be delivered against that contract, when it can be delivered and how it can be delivered. There is no ambiguity.

Credit and margin

Let us return to the would-be gold miner. Assume that the miner sells a contract to a speculator. The miner and the speculator do not take each other's credit risk, because both take that of the clearing house. But equally, doesn't this mean that the clearing house has to take their credit risk?

The clearing house does not deal directly with the end-users, such as the gold miner. Clearing houses deal with brokers, who deal with the end-users. Clearing houses protect themselves by insisting that brokers take from their clients *margin*, a good-faith deposit of cash or bonds. The brokers must then post that margin at the clearing house.

So, the miner sells one contract. Let us imagine that this contract is the Sep 2001 gold contract, traded on COMEX, and it is sold at a price of $275. The price is quoted per troy ounce, but one contract is for 100 troy ounces.

There is an *initial margin* set by the clearing house, intended to be enough to cover the clearing house against a day's move or so. For the COMEX gold contract, the clearing house currently sets the initial margin to be $13.50 per troy ounce, a total of $1350 on one contract. This initial margin protects the broker, and hence the clearing house, against a combination of a default and a change in the price of up to $13.50.

What would happen if the price were to rise by $3? Recall that the miner is *short*, that is, overall the miner has sold contracts and so in effect owns a negative number of contracts. An initial margin of $13.50 had been paid. Allowing for the $3 loss, only $10.50 of that initial margin remains. So the miner must top up the margin by paying a *variation margin* or *maintenance margin* of $3 per troy ounce to the clearing house, effectively paying losses immediately.

The speculator is *long* a Sep 2001 gold contract at $275, and like the miner paid an initial margin of $13.50. But when the price rose $3, the speculator made a $3 profit and so became overmargined, and hence is allowed to top down the margin by that $3.

So the clearing house simply transmitted the miner's payment of $3 per troy ounce to the speculator. The effect of the variation margin payments is that losses are paid and gains are realised immediately, with losers paying the winners (via the clearing house) in cash almost immediately. This is known as *mark-to-market*.

The payment of variation margin means that everybody starts the day in the same effective position. A trader who bought at $260 and a trader who bought at $275 each start the day as if they had bought at $278. The cumulative profits up to that moment (of $18 and $3) have already been received.

So what happens at delivery? Let us assume that the price holds steady at $278 until delivery. At delivery, those who are short deliver gold, and those who are long pay $278 per troy ounce. This means that a trader who bought the contract at $260 will have paid a total of $260 per troy ounce: $278 at expiry, less the $18 received in the form of variation margin during the life of the contract.

When the outstanding position is closed, either by letting it run to expiry, or by repurchasing it, the initial margin of $1350 per contract is returned, with interest.

Cash settlement

Gold is a convenient thing to deliver. It comes in the form of durable ingots with a high value per unit volume and per unit weight, so it is reasonably cheap to store millions of dollars' worth of gold. Ingots are stored in a vault; delivering an ingot usually consists of no more than delivering a depository receipt.

But delivering oil would be messier. Brent crude (crude oil from the North Sea's Brent oilfield) only comes in supertanker loads. Delivering 1000 barrels, the size of a single futures contract on the International Petroleum Exchange in London, would be highly inconvenient and hence expensive. So a different delivery mechanism is used instead.

At expiry the exchange observes and records the price at which physical oil is trading. This is deemed to be the final price of the contract. All those owning contracts (all longs) are deemed to sell their positions at this price, and all those who have sold (all shorts) are deemed to buy back their positions at this price. So if someone buys December 2001 Brent at $25, and at expiry Brent crude costs $29.50 per barrel, the profit would total $4.50 per barrel, and all of this would have been paid in the form of variation margin.

If a market participant wanted physical delivery, this could easily be constructed. Someone who wants delivery of crude oil, and who had bought the contract at $25 per barrel, would take one extra step: to purchase oil in the market when the contract expires. The total cost of the oil would be $25 ($29.50 to buy the oil, minus the $4.50 profit received in the form of variation margin).

Contracts that have this form of delivery are said to be *cash-settled*. Cash settlement relies crucially on having a method of determining the final price that is fair, transparent and cannot be manipulated.

Cash-settling other contracts

The above futures contract was on Brent crude oil. This is because the final value of the contract was the cost of Brent. But this cost is only a number: the same mechanism could be used to make a futures contract on any number.

That number could be the price of a barrel of oil. It could be the value of an equity index, such as the S&P 500 or the FTSE 100. It could be an interest rate or a formula involving an interest rate. Indeed, it could be any number at all, provided the method of determining that number has been specified in advance.

As an example, let us consider the FTSE 100 contract, traded on the London International Financial Futures Exchange (LIFFE). This settles against the FTSE 100, the equity market index consisting of the UK's 100 largest companies. The contract specification describes the calculation of the expiry value, known as the exchange delivery settlement price (EDSP), as follows:

> The EDSP is based on the average values of the FTSE 100 Index every 15 seconds between (and including) 10:10 and 10:30 (London time) on the Last Trading Day. Of the 81 measured values, the highest 12 and lowest 12 will be discarded and the remaining 57 will be averaged to calculate the EDSP. Where necessary, the calculation will be rounded to the nearest half index point.

The EDSP is thus determined in a manner that excludes transient errors or spikes in the prices. This method is transparent, robust and difficult to manipulate.

Among the most heavily traded futures contracts are the interest-rate futures; settling these requires a transparent and non-manipulable method of determining a short-term interest rate. The method used is known as a *fixing*, and the interest-rate fixings are of enormous importance to financial markets. They are used not only in interest-rate futures, but also in many other heavily traded financial instruments.

The fixings

The fixings started in 1985, under the auspices of the British Bankers' Association (BBA). The BBA fixes *Libor*, the London Inter-Bank Offered Rate. At 11 am each London business day, the BBA asks sixteen banks for the rate at which that bank can borrow USD for 3 months. Each of these sixteen banks is asked to

> contribute the rate at which it could borrow funds, were it to do so by asking for and then accepting inter-bank offers in reasonable market size just prior to 1100.

This is the rate at which interbank money is offered, for a deposit 'governed by the laws of England and Wales'.

Sixteen banks submit rates; the highest four rates and the lowest four rates are discarded, and the central eight averaged. This average is the official *fixing* of USD 3-month Libor.

Indeed, the BBA asks not just for 3-month US dollars. It *fixes* 1-day, 1-week, 2-week, 1-month, 2-, 3-, 4-, 5-, 6-, 7-, 8-, 9-, 10-, 11- and 12-month Libor in each of USD, EUR, GBP, JPY, CHF, AUD and CAD. In some of the smaller currencies fewer than sixteen banks are consulted, but the principle is the same.

This process is well designed. If one of the sixteen banks were to attempt to manipulate the fixing by submitting a falsely high rate, then that bank's submission would become one of the discarded highest four, and hence not used in the average. Besides being futile, it would be illegal to attempt to manipulate the fixing, but the design of the process ensures that those contributing the rates aren't tempted to try.

Other banking associations also conduct fixings. At 11 am Frankfurt time, the European Banking Federation surveys a large number of banks about the cost of borrowing euros, in maturities of 1 week and the twelve monthly maturities out to 1 year. The top and bottom 15% of quotations are discarded, and the central quotations averaged to produce the fixing of *Euribor*.

The Japanese banking association produces the fixing of *Tibor*, the cost of borrowing yen in Tokyo. There is active trading in both Tibor and JPY Libor, and also in the difference between them. The difference is traded because the Tibor fixing panel contains more Japanese and fewer US and European banks than the JPY Libor panel. Japanese banks are currently deemed to be a worse credit risk than non-Japanese banks, and hence they have a higher cost of borrowing, so Tibor typically fixes higher than JPY Libor.

Other banking associations produce fixings of local currency interbank interest rates: Stibor in Stockholm, Cibor in Copenhagen, Wibor in Warsaw, and others elsewhere. A generic term for the interest rate fixings is IBOR, which encompasses the various Libors, Euribor, Tibor, etc.

As an aside, note that the rate at which a bank is willing to accept a deposit is colloquially known as Libid, as it reflects the bid rather than the offered rate. Limid is the average of Libor and Libid. Unlike Libor, there is no formal fixing of Libid, but it is typically one-sixteenth to one-eighth of a percent below Libor.

The 3-month interest-rate future

So we now know how futures work, how cash-settled futures work, and how interbank interest rates are fixed. These can be put together into a 3-month interest-rate future. This is simply a cash-settled futures contract that settles against 100 minus the 3-month IBOR fixing in the appropriate currency. For most currencies the expiry date is the Monday before the third Wednesday of the delivery month. This day of the month is known as the *IMM date*, after the International Monetary Exchange, on which these futures were first listed.

So the March 2006 USD interest-rate future settles against 100 minus the 3-month USD Libor fixing on Monday 13 March 2006. At the close of business (cob) on 16 February 2001, this contract was trading at a price of 93.675. And hence at the close on this day the market's expectation for 3-month USD Libor on 13 March 2006 was 100 − 93.675, which equals 6.325%.

Why 100 minus the IBOR? Recall that as the price of a bond increases, its yield decreases. Using 100 minus IBOR ensures that interest-rate futures have the same directionality, with an increase in price being a decrease in yield.

We have already said that, for most currencies, the expiry date is the IMM date, the Monday before the third Wednesday of the delivery month. The exception is GBP, for which the expiry date is the third Wednesday itself. The motivation behind this is easy: the sterling money market has T+0 settlement, the others T+2. So for all currencies the futures contract refers to the cost of deposit that starts on the third Wednesday of the expiry month. And why the third Wednesday at all? Perhaps because 3 months after a third Wednesday is never a weekend or a public holiday.

The most liquid contracts are those expiring in the last month of the quarter, March, June, September and December. There is little activity in the contracts that expire in the *serial months*, i.e. in the first and second month of each quarter. In USD only, it is also possible to trade contracts that settle against 1-month Libor.

Price action

The next two charts illustrate some actual price action. We start by looking at the state of the USD yield curve on 20 January 1994. The US was in the process of emerging from the recession of the early 1990s, by the end of which the official interest rate of the US Federal Reserve was 3%. During 1993 the cost of 3-month inter-bank dollars (3-month USD Libor) had drifted between 3.1875% and 3.5625%, and the fixing on 20 January 1994 was exactly 3.25%.

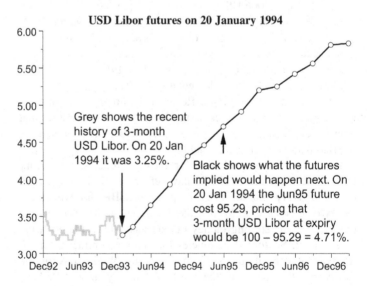

USD Libor futures on 20 January 1994

Grey shows the recent history of 3-month USD Libor. On 20 Jan 1994 it was 3.25%.

Black shows what the futures implied would happen next. On 20 Jan 1994 the Jun95 future cost 95.29, pricing that 3-month USD Libor at expiry would be 100 − 95.29 = 4.71%.

So much for the past, the financial markets also tell us what is expected to happen in the future: the USD interest-rate futures were predicting that dollar Libor would rise gently from this 3.25% level. On 20 January 1994 the Jun94 contract cost 96.35, a rate of 3.65%. Equivalently, on 20 January 1994 the market was pricing that 3-month USD Libor would be 3.65% on 13 June 1994. On the same day, the Jun95 contract (with an expiry date of 19 June 1995) cost 95.29, a rate of 4.71%. All of this is illustrated in the chart on page 44.

So, to recap, 3-month USD Libor had been steady between 3.1875% and 3.5625%, but was expected to rise over the next several years at an average pace of just under 1% per year.

What actually happened next? The market was hopelessly wrong. In fact, the Federal Reserve started raising rates, immediately and fast. By 13 June 1994, 3-month USD Libor had reached 4.5625%, some 91.25bp more than the market had been expecting in January, and by 21 July 1994 the fixing was at

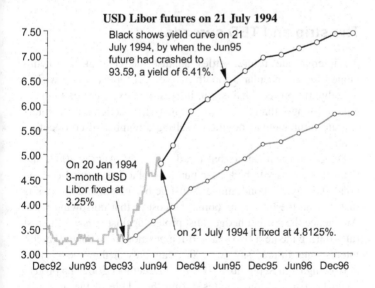

USD Libor futures on 21 July 1994

Black shows yield curve on 21 July 1994, by when the Jun95 future had crashed to 93.59, a yield of 6.41%.

On 20 Jan 1994 3-month USD Libor fixed at 3.25%

on 21 July 1994 it fixed at 4.8125%.

4.8125%. By this date in July the Jun95 contract (which had not yet expired) had changed from implying 4.71% (i.e. costing 95.29), to implying 6.41% (i.e. the price had dropped to 93.59). The chart on page 45 shows the state of play on 21 July 1994, overlaid on that of 20 January. Bond and interest-rate futures in the US, UK and Europe all plunged during 1994, which is why this example was chosen.

There are other features to note in this chart. In January 1994 the difference between the Sep94 and Dec94 contracts was 0.38. Rephrased, in January 1994 the market was pricing a rise in interest rates of 38bp (0.38%) between the expiries of the Sep94 and Dec94 contracts. By July this difference had increased to 69bp: the Sep94–Dec94 curve is said to have steepened from 38bp to 69bp. But in contrast the Jun96–Jun97 curve flattened from 54bp to 40bp. In summary the whole curve sold off (a decrease in price being an increase in yield), but some parts of the curve steepened and other parts flattened.

The strip and TED spreads

An interest-rate future settles against the cost of borrowing money for a particular 3-month period. Yet typically one wishes to hedge (to protect against) an interest rate exposure that covers a period longer than 3 months, so many transactions in the interest-rate futures entail buying or selling a number of consecutive contracts.

For example, imagine that the date is now August 2002, and that it is necessary to hedge the purchase of a 2-year fixed-coupon bond. To buy the bond, money must be borrowed, and the risk is that, during the life of the bond, the cost of that borrowing rises. And hence the correct hedge must protect against a rise in interest rates during the next two years. But a position in just one 3-month interest-rate future, say Sep2002, can only hedge the cost of borrowing from September 2002 until December 2002. To protect against a rise in interest rates during the whole of the next two years would require selling some number of each of the *front* eight contracts: Sep2002, Dec2002, Mar2003, Jun2003, Sep2003, Dec2003, Mar2004 and Jun2004. One would then have traded a *strip* of contracts: this is an entirely different use of the word 'strip' to that explained in Chapter 2.

Buying a bond and selling the interest-rate futures is known as buying the *TED spread*. The term originated in the US: the T is for Treasury, the ED for the eurodollar contracts, which are the interest-rate futures settling against 3-month USD Libor.

Buying the TED entails buying a bond, obtaining the money to do this by borrowing short-term, and selling futures to lock in the cost of rolling over that borrowing. It is therefore possible to calculate a profit or loss for this trade, by assuming that the subsequent borrowings are at the rate at which the futures settle (i.e. at the IBOR in the relevant currency).

Alternatively, one could calculate how much cheaper or dearer the futures would have to be for the trade to break even. This represents how much more or less the bond yields than the strip. A government bond will typically yield less than Libor, and may well trade at a TED of –40bp; one might say that it yields Libor minus 40bp. In contrast, a bond issued by a weak corporation will typically yield more than Libor, and may well have a TED of more than +100bp. TED spreads are actively traded in dollars, euros and sterling.

Arbitrage

We have discussed at length the specification of futures contracts, which determines what is delivered or how the final price is fixed. But this does not explain why, before delivery, there should be a close linkage between the price of the underlying and the price of the future.

Let us return to the example of gold and imagine that a futures contract was trading expensively. An *arbitrageur* would take advantage of this. The arbitrageur would buy *spot gold* (i.e.

gold for immediate delivery) and simultaneously sell the futures contract. The money for buying the gold would be borrowed, incurring an interest charge, and there would also be the cost of warehousing the gold. However, if the difference between the price of the future and the spot price were larger than these costs, there would be a guaranteed profit.

The reverse trade is also possible. If the futures contract were trading too cheaply, an arbitrageur could borrow gold and sell it, simultaneously buying the futures contract. Selling spot gold versus buying the future would prevent the future from becoming too cheap.

The fact that arbitrageurs can do a *cash-and-carry trade* or *reverse cash-and-carry trade* is what keeps the contract near its fair value. Arbitrageurs are active, or at least willing to be active, in almost all futures contracts.

Some trading jargon

When trading futures there is a constraint on wording that is widely and precisely followed. If buying 100 contracts, the price being 74, one would say '74 for 100'. If selling, one would say '100 at 74'. Adherence to this is very strict; do not say 'buy 100 at 74', because the preposition 'at' is used only when selling, never when buying. Buying is always 'price for volume', selling is always 'volume at price'. This precise usage is to mini-mise communication errors; nobody wants to discover that an order to buy was interpreted as an order to sell.

Unless otherwise specified, an order to buy or sell is *good* until the close of business or until cancelled. For example, an order 'June Bunds, sell 200 at 74' might be met with a response 'work-ing 200 at 74', quickly followed by 'sold 150, working 50'. The order to sell 50 more contracts at 74 would remain in the system until the close of the day, or until cancelled. However, a number of variations on this have become so standard that they are referred to by abbreviation:

- GTC is good till cancelled. A GTC order may be worked over many days.
- OCO is one cancels other. If two orders are given and one is filled, the other is cancelled. For example, 'June Bunds pay 74 for 200, Sep Bunds pay 87 for 200, OCO', might be met by '87 paid for 200 in Sep, June order cancelled'.
- FOK is fill or kill. It says that as much as possible of the order should be done now, the rest cancelled. So an order 'sell 200 at 74 FOK' might be followed by a reply '150 at 74 filled, 50 unabled'.
- MOC is market on close. So '73 for 200 MOC' means pay 73 for 200, but just before the close, pay whatever is the prevailing market price for the remainder of the order. MOO, a less common variant, means market on open.
- Stop orders are usually used to take losses. Imagine that the market is now trading at 74. A trader who is long might leave an order 'sell 1000 at 65 on stop, limit 60'. This says that if the market should trade down to 65, then the broker is to sell 1000 contracts, at a price no worse than 60.

There is also jargon for the names of contract expiries. If the date is now August 2002, the Sep02 contract is the September contract nearest to expiry, and is called *front Sep*. The following September contract, Sep03, is called *red Sep*, because the names of the second-year contracts were in red on the price board of the IMM. Third-year contracts are green and fourth-year contracts are blue.

When computers started to be used in finance, single-character codes for expiry months were introduced to save on limited screen space. These codes are still used: H is March, M is June, U is September and Z is December. There is no obvious pattern, but as they are widely used, they have to be learnt. So in August 2002 the Dec03 contract might be called either 'red Dec' or 'Z3' (the '3' being the last digit of the year).

Summary

- Futures contracts allow trading without taking counterparty credit risk.
- Positions net: a buy and a sell cancel properly, without any residual risk.
- Upon initiating a position, an initial margin must be paid to protect the broker and clearing house against default by the client.
- Subsequent losses must be paid immediately, profits are taken immediately.
- Some futures contracts are physically delivered, others are cash-settled.
- The price of a future is defined by what is deliverable or by how the final value is determined; this is always specified precisely.
- Arbitrage keeps the spot and futures prices in synchrony.
- The 3-month interest-rate futures are traded versus bonds; the price of the package of bonds and futures is called the TED spread.
- Buying is always price for volume; selling is always volume at price.
- H is March, M is June, U is September and Z is December; second-year contracts are red, third-year contracts are green.

Chapter 4

Swaps

Introduction

Nearly all tradable debt is in one of two forms: fixed-rate or floating-rate. Fixed-rate debt pays coupons of fixed size, whereas floating-rate debt pays coupons that are set using a short-term interest rate, usually Libor or another IBOR.

A floating-rate asset can be likened to a deposit in a savings account at a high-street bank. Assume that the deposit is of 100 currency units, and that the interest is withdrawn or paid into a different account. Such saving accounts pay a floating rate of interest, sometimes higher and sometimes lower. However, at any time the account can be closed and the original 100 units of money withdrawn, so in effect the price of the account is constant at 100.

A fixed-rate bond is the opposite. It pays a fixed coupon, say 7%, for the life of the bond. If this is deemed generous, the market price of the bond will be above 100; if miserly, below. A change in yield is a change in price.

In practice the market price of a floating-rate bond is not exactly constant, as it is affected by changes in the creditworthiness of the issuer, and by other variables. Nonetheless, the price of fixed-rate

51

debt is typically much more volatile than the price of floating-rate debt. This is illustrated in the next chart, which shows the price history of two gilts, both issued by the British government and both maturing in late 2001. Observe that the price of the fixed-coupon gilt varies much more than the price of the floating-rate gilt.

Price history of the 7% gilt 2001 and the floating-rate gilt 2001

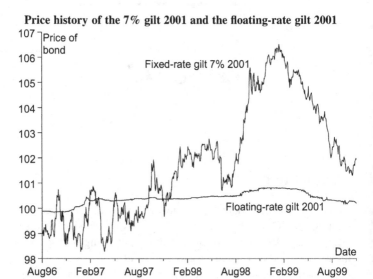

Some investors do not want the price volatility associated with a fixed-rate asset. These investors prefer to buy assets that pay floating-rate coupons. Banks are a typical example: they borrow from their depositors at a floating rate and they want their lending to match.

So what can a would-be investor do if the borrower has issued fixed-rate debt? This is not an uncommon situation: the over-whelming majority of government debt is fixed-rate. Clearly it would be useful to have some form of conversion mechanism by which a series of fixed-rate payments can be exchanged or swapped for a series of floating-rate payments. Given such a conversion mechanism, an investor buying fixed-rate debt and swapping it to floating rate could then think about the all-in cost of the floating-rate asset; that is, the cost of the bond plus the cost of the conversion mechanism.

Other investors, particularly those that buy long-dated bonds, such as insurance companies and pension funds, prefer fixed-rate debt. How could such investors lend money to an institution that wanted to borrow money at a floating rate? The same conversion mechanism could be used: the borrower issues fixed-rate debt and then executes a second transaction to convert this liability from fixed-rate to floating-rate.

This mechanism is called an *interest-rate swap* (IRS) or just a plain *swap*. The existence of swaps broadens the choices available to issuers and investors.

An example

Let us consider the position of an issuer who wants to borrow money at a floating rate. This is typical of many financial institutions, from ordinary high-street banks to the World Bank.

The issuer could issue floating-rate debt, in which case no swap is needed. Alternatively, it could issue fixed-rate debt and do a side deal with an investment bank to swap its obligation to make fixed-rate payments into an obligation to make floating-rate payments.

This would work as follows. The borrower issues a fixed-rate bond. The side deal converts this fixed-rate bond to floating rate, which is what the borrower wanted to issue. Under the terms of the side deal, the borrower receives fixed-rate payments from an investment bank, to whom it makes floating-rate payments. This exchange of payments continues for the life of the bond.

The borrower's net position is that it pays a floating rate: it pays fixed coupons on the bond, receives fixed coupons as a result of the swap with the investment bank, and pays floating coupons to the investment bank, also as a result of the swap.

**A fixed-rate bond swapped to floating: cashflows at issue,
during its life and at maturity**

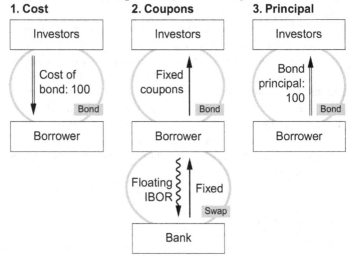

The cashflows of the whole arrangement are summarised in the diagram. They occur in three sets. The first is at the start, when the investors pay for the bond. At this stage the swap plays no role.

The second is during the life of the bond, when the borrower pays fixed coupons to the investors, and exchanges fixed and floating coupons with the investment bank. As an example, imagine that the bond has a coupon of 6.25% and that the fixed leg of the swap is at 5.50%. Then the borrower would be paying 6.25% to the investors, receiving 5.50% from the bank, and paying IBOR to the bank. Its overall cost of funds would therefore be IBOR + 75bp. Finally, at maturity, the borrower repays the principal of the bond.

In diagrams such as these it is conventional to show fixed payments with a straight line and floating payments with a wavy line. Also, it is usual to show only those parts in which there are any cashflows relating to the swap.

So a borrower who wants floating-rate liabilities can choose to issue a floating-rate bond or to issue a swapped fixed-coupon bond. If investors particularly demand bonds of one type, then the cheapest method of borrowing will be to issue the type that the investors prefer.

Asset swaps

We have seen that a swap can be useful to an issuer. Equally, swaps can be useful to investors. Imagine that a company has issued a fixed-coupon 10-year bond. An owner of this bond faces two risks: that 10-year interest rates might rise, and that the credit of the issuer might deteriorate. Swaps allow these two risks to be separated. An investor could buy the bond and separately pay fixed (and hence receive floating) on a swap.

Cashflows for an asset swap

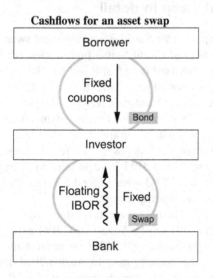

The investor's net position is that of a floating-rate bond. The investor has hedged away the interest-rate risk of the bond and is left with the residual credit risk.

This package of bond and swap is very similar to the TED spread (Chapter 3); it is known as an *asset swap*. The reverse position, being short the bond and receiving on the swap, is a *reverse asset swap*.

Asset swaps are very actively traded, particularly for government bonds. Indeed, the level of government asset swaps is so important to the interest-rate markets that the yield of a government bond is often quoted as the price of the asset swap. So the yield might be described as Libor – 78bp or swaps – 78bp, rather than as an absolute yield in percentage points.

Note though that there are several different methods of calculating asset swaps. Although they are all similar in principle, the resulting quotations do differ, particularly for bonds with a price far from 100.

A typical swap in detail

As an example, let us consider a hypothetical swap between J. P. Morgan (JPM) and Credit Suisse First Boston (CSFB). Suppose JPM is to receive fixed from CSFB and pay floating to CSFB. The swap is in USD, for 10 years and is to start on 15 August 2007. We also assume that the fixed rate, which is the *price* of the swap, is 6% and that both the fixed and floating payments are semi-annual.

The payments on the swap are exactly the same as the payments from an exchange of deposits. So let us consider what the payments would be if JPM were to lend $100 to CSFB for 10 years at 6%, and CSFB were to lend $100 to JPM for the same period of time at floating Libor.

First, we consider the payments resulting from JPM's fixed-rate deposit with CSFB. On 15 August 2007 JPM pays $100 to CSFB. Every 6 months thereafter, CSFB pays interest at a rate of 6% to JPM, and on the maturity day, 15 August 2017, makes the final interest payment and returns the principal of $100.

Second, we consider the payments resulting from CSFB's floating-rate deposit with JPM. Initially, on 15 August 2007, CSFB pays $100 to JPM. Subsequently, JPM pays floating Libor to CSFB. So, on 15 February 2008 JPM would pay to CSFB the interest on a 6-month deposit, calculated using the Libor fixing on 13 August 2007. Why 13 August rather than 15 August? Because the interest rate on a USD deposit is agreed 2 business days before the start of a deposit period: US dollars are $T+2$. The last interest payment and the principal of $100 are paid on the maturity day of 15 August 2017.

Now let us add together these two series of cashflows. At the start, each paid the other $100; these payments cancel. At maturity, each paid the other $100; these also cancel. Throughout the life of the swap, every 6 months, each paid the other interest; one paying fixed, the other floating. These interest payments are netted and only the difference is transmitted.

These payments constitute an interest-rate swap; a swap entails the exchange of fixed-rate and floating-rate deposits. The principal amounts at the start of a swap cancel, as do those at the end, and therefore they are not exchanged.

Let us restate the cashflows. The swap starts with the two parties observing the fixing of 6-month USD Libor on 13 August 2007. This Libor refers to the price of a deposit that runs from 15 August 2007 to 15 February 2008, and the interest payable is calculated. The parties also calculate the interest that would be payable if the deposit rate were 6%. The two parties exchange these interest payments on 15 February 2008. Only the difference is transmitted.

The next coupon period runs from 15 February 2008 to 15 August 2008. The floating rate is fixed two days before the start, on 13 February 2008, and the interest on a deposit at that rate is calculated. The parties also calculate the interest on a deposit at 6%. Again, these are exchanged. These exchanges continue until 15 August 2017, the cashflow payable on this date being determined on 13 February 2017.

Note that there is no requirement for an underlying bond or borrowing. Swaps are often used to convert an asset or a liability to or from fixed-rate, but this is not necessary. Swaps are often traded separately, without any underlying loan.

Credit risk in swaps

In the previous example we saw how a trader of credit risk, but not of interest-rate risk, might use a swap to hedge the interest-rate risk in a corporate bond. But swaps are not devoid of all credit risk, it is just that they entail very much less credit risk than a loan or a deposit.

If a bank lends a customer $100 for 2 years and the customer goes bust during that time, the bank is $100 out of pocket. But if a bank trades a 2-year interest-rate swap, there will be two years in which cashflows are exchanged. The size of these cashflows is the difference between the fixed and floating rates; typically this might be of the order of ±1% each year. So, for a 2-year swap, the payments might only total ±2% of the nominal amount of the swap. The swap payments are very much smaller than the payments on a loan, and therefore the credit risk is much less.

For a longer-dated swap, the risk might be more than ±2%. But whatever the maturity, the credit risk will be much less than for a bond of similar maturity and coupon.

One other factor particularly affects the credit risk in a swap. Imagine that the curve is steeply positive: short-dated interest rates are low, longer-dated interest rates are much higher. We saw an example of this in Chapter 4; the USD yield curve was positive during 1994—the market believed that interest rates were set to rise. If a bank pays fixed on a swap when the curve is positive, the bank's early payments will be outwards, when it pays fixed against receiving the currently low level of the Libor fixings. However, the bank expects that the later payments, after interest rates have risen, will be in its favour. Of course, the market price of the swap (the interest rate on the fixed leg) is such that the estimated positive and negative payment streams have the same present value. Nonetheless, the swap entails the bank paying money early in the life of the swap and having it returned later in the life of the swap. To part with money now and have it returned later is equivalent to making a loan. The size of this loan may be only a small fraction of the notional size of the swap, but it is still a loan and therefore a cause of credit exposure.

The price of the swap should therefore make allowance for the possibility of a default during its life. So, in theory, the price quoted to a client should depend on that client's creditworthiness, and the portfolio of transactions already outstanding with that client, as well as the cashflows in the swap. However, while it is relatively easy to measure the current exposure to each counter-party, and to keep track of the regulators' definition of risk, it is very difficult to calculate the expected average loss caused by possible future defaults.

Trading jargon

Let us return to our hypothetical example in which J. P. Morgan is receiving 6% fixed from and paying floating to CSFB for 10 years starting on 15 August 2007, with a nominal size of USD 100 million. This might be described as JPM receives 6% from CSFB for 10 years out of 15 Aug 07 in USD 100 million.

If someone receives on a swap, this always refers to the fixed leg. So *to receive* is to receive fixed and pay floating. The opposite is to pay; *to pay* is to pay fixed and to receive floating. So the receiving or the paying always refers to the fixed leg of the swap.

Other swaps terminology is more confusing. Traders of most things, including bonds and swaps, use the terms 'buy' and 'sell'. And if a bond trader buys a bond, that trader wants the price to go up, which is the same as wanting the yield to go down.

But interest-rate swaps are always quoted in yield. And when a trader buys a swap, the trader wants the yield to go up. So buying a swap is taking risk in the opposite direction to buying a bond. Rephrased, one might buy a bond, and then hedge by buying a swap.

In both bonds and swaps, to 'take' or 'lift' means the same as to buy, and to 'give' or 'hit' means to sell. The phrase 'I buy' is often abbreviated to 'Mine!', usually shouted, and 'I sell' to 'Yours!', and again the shouting seems to be compulsory. To summarise:

Bonds		Swaps	
		Receive	Pay
Buy	Sell	Sell	Buy
Bid	Ask or Offer	Ask or Offer	Bid
Take	Give	Give	Take
Lift	Hit	Hit	Lift
Mine!	Yours!	Yours!	Mine!
Lend	Borrow	Lend	Borrow

Those looking for a happy moral in this confusing tale should note that, in the swap market at least, to give is to receive.

Swaps and interest-rate futures

A swap is very similar to a strip of interest-rate futures. For example, the profit and loss exposure in receiving (fixed, of course) on a 3-year swap is very similar to that of buying an appropriate number of each of the first three years of interest-rate futures. However, there are a few differences:

- Interest-rate futures are marked to market. Profits and losses are transferred almost immediately; all futures contracts have daily flows of variation margin. By contrast, swaps have such margin flows only by special agreement between the counterparties. Therefore an end-user, typically a company not constantly active in financial markets, may well prefer a swap, as its cash management department will not want to risk suddenly having to find or invest significant sums of money.
- Because interest-rate futures have a daily mark-to-market, the credit exposure is nearly zero. In contrast, swaps can entail substantial credit exposure to the counterparty.

- Interest-rate futures in most currencies expire only on IMM dates, so there is a restricted choice of expiry dates. In contrast, one can trade a swap with an arbitrary set of cashflows that fix on any mutually agreed date, and that fix against an IBOR of any term (though 1, 3 and 6 months are usual). Swaps are flexible.
- Swaps trade for much longer maturities than interest-rate futures. USD interest-rate futures exist out to 10 years, and are easily traded in reasonable size out to about 5 years. EUR and GBP futures exist only out to 5 years, though they are very *illiquid*, difficult to trade, beyond 3 years; this cutoff is shorter in JPY, and even shorter in AUD, CAD and CHF. In contrast, the 30-year swap markets are active in the big four currencies, and it is possible to trade out to 50 years.
- The price of an interest-rate future is much more transparent than the price of a swap. Futures are all exchange-traded, and the price and size of each transaction is published within a few seconds. Swaps are not; if two counterparties transact a swap, nobody else need ever know, let alone promptly.
- There is a very small difference in pricing between swaps and interest-rate futures caused mostly by the value of the daily mark-to-market. The cause of this difference is known as *convexity*, most of which is attributable to the *financing bias*. However, the highly mathematical details of the calculation lie beyond the scope of this book, except to remark that for futures with less than two years to expiry, the difference is usually worth less than 1bp.
- Finally, in some jurisdictions there can be differences in tax, or in the timing of tax payments.

Myth and reality

The swap market appears to be huge. The Bank for International Settlements conducts a survey of market liquidity every three years, and its April 1998 survey showed that typical daily turnover in the swaps and similar markets was then $155 billion, and that a total of $40 trillion swaps were outstanding.

$155 billion may seem to be a large quantity of money—more than the annual gross domestic product of sub-Saharan Africa. But this enormously overstates the actual risk in the system. For example, imagine that two counterparties have three swaps outstanding. One party is paying $100 million 10 years, and is receiving $50 million 8 years and $50 million 12 years. These swaps have almost offsetting risks, so the overall risk is very much smaller than the nominal sizes of the swaps. A typical weekly profit or loss for such a position might be ±$100,000, only 0.05% of the total sizes of the swaps.

This mismatch of scale may be part of the reason why the derivative markets, consisting mostly of swaps and futures, are misunderstood. Using swaps it is indeed possible to trade the interest-rate risk on large sums of money, but the total risk outstanding is far less than the headline number suggests.

Summary

- A swap is effectively an exchange of deposits, with much reduced credit risk.
- Swaps allow interest-rate risk to be transferred between parties, and they are used by both issuers and investors.
- A swap is much less credit-intensive than a one-sided deposit, but it is not free of credit risk.
- Asset swaps are actively traded, and the yield of a bond is often quoted relative to the swap.

Chapter 5

Options

Introduction

Let us return to the gold miner of Chapter 3, whose mining and purifying costs are $250 per troy ounce. The gold miner could lock in the sale price of gold, by selling gold 1 year forward or by selling gold futures. Either would be sensible. But now let us assume the miner has a strong belief that the price of gold is going up. The miner wants to keep the upside if gold rallies, but wants protection just in case the price of gold falls below $250. In other words, what is needed is a financial instrument that allows the miner to sell gold at $250 if it falls below that price, but to keep the gold if it doesn't.

Puts and calls

There is such a financial instrument, named a *put option*. It gives the holder the right, but not the obligation, to sell a specific amount of the underlying instrument at a predetermined *strike price* on or before an *expiry date*. In this example the underlying is gold, the strike price is $250; and let us say that the expiry is 1 year from the purchase date.

So the miner buys a 1-year $250 put on gold. What happens at the end of the year, when expiry is imminent? If gold then costs more than $250 in the market, it would be better to sell gold into the market at more than $250 than to sell gold at $250 by *exercising* the put option. So if gold costs more than $250, the option is worthless and should be discarded.

But if gold costs less than $250, it would be better to sell gold at $250 than to sell gold at the sub-$250 market price. In this case the option is worth $1 for each $1 that gold costs less than $250. If gold costs $200 at the end of the year, the option will be worth $50.

A put option, a put, gives the holder the right to sell an asset at a predetermined price on or before the expiry date. Its twin gives the holder the right to buy and it is known as a *call option*. Just before expiry, one would choose to exercise a call option if the price of the underlying were above that of the strike, in which case the call would be worth $1 for every $1 that the price was above. And if the price of the underlying were below the strike, the option would be discarded. The small *hockey stick* diagrams illustrate the payoffs as a function of the market price of the underlying instrument.

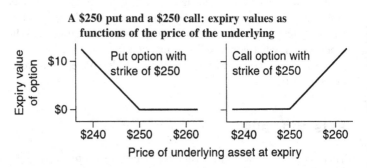

A $250 put and a $250 call: expiry values as functions of the price of the underlying

Of course, the protection given by an option has a cost.

What is the option worth?

Let us return to the 1-year $250 put on gold. What is this put option worth? At expiry this option can always be thrown away, so it can't cost less than zero. And at expiry it might have some value, possibly a large value, so before expiry it must have some cost—a cost that reflects the probability of it being worth something, and the expected size of that something.

Let us assume that gold for delivery in 1 year now costs $275, and that the price of this gold future changes very little. Then a put option with a strike of $250 will be worth hardly anything, perhaps as much as $1 or maybe less.

Alternatively, let us assume again that gold for delivery in 1 year now costs $275, but that this price moves considerably every day, sometimes by a few dollars, occasionally by a few tens of dollars. Now the probability is much higher that this option will be worth something at expiry. It is even plausible that at expiry the option could be worth many tens of dollars. In this case the put option will cost much more, perhaps several tens of dollars.

As a third example, let us assume that gold for delivery in 1 year costs as little as $100, and again that this price hardly ever moves. Then a $250 put is highly likely to be worth very close to $150 at expiry, which occurs in 1 year's time. If interest rates are 6%, then $150 in 1 year is worth $141.51 now, which is therefore the price of the option.

From these three examples we can see that the price of a put option depends on the current forward price, on the variability or volatility of the forward price, and on prevailing interest rates. So:

- Lower forward gives a higher put price
- Higher volatility gives a higher put price
- Lower interest rates marginally increase the price of the option

Similar reasoning applies to a call option, which gives the holder the right to buy, except that a higher price of the underlying means a higher price of the call option.

Combinations

Options are often traded in combinations, containing a mixture of calls and puts, of the same or different strikes. The next diagram shows the payoffs for two such combinations. The *straddle* consists of a long position in a call and a long position in a put with the same strike. It has its minimum value if prices settle at the strike, and it does best if prices end a long way from the strike—in either direction.

The *call spread*, also known as a *bull spread*, is constructed by buying a call and selling a higher-strike call. The owner of a call spread wants prices to be high, but the risk to be limited. To reduce the cost of this limited risk, the maximum gain is also capped.

There are many other combinations and some of them have evocative names such as strangle, butterfly, condor, ladder and one-by-two.

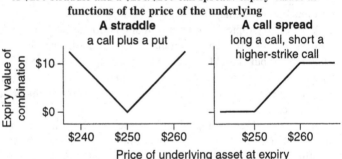

A $250 straddle and a $250/$260 call spread: expiry values as functions of the price of the underlying

Underlyings

So far we have looked only at gold options. But options also trade on many different instruments, including metals, oil, foreign exchange, bonds, swaps and many different futures contracts.

For example, a British exporter who sells to the eurozone might be concerned that the euro might fall against the pound. For the exporter, a weaker euro means either lower sterling profit margins per item sold, or a higher euro price and hence a lower volume of sales. To protect against this, the exporter might buy an option, allowing (but not compelling) a sale of EUR and a purchase of GBP. Such an instrument would be known as an EUR put GBP call, as it gives the right to sell euros in exchange for sterling. If sterling soars then the option protects, but if sterling plummets then the exporter can keep the additional sterling revenue. Which-ever happens, the exporter must pay for the option.

Options, like futures, can be physically delivered or cash-settled. If a physically delivered option on gold is exercised, then the gold changes hands. But if a cash-settled option on gold is exercised, then the price of the underlying is observed, the value of the option is calculated, and this amount is paid to the holder.

Embedded options

Options often appear in disguise, embedded in other instruments. Consider a *capped floater*. This is a floating-rate note (FRN) that pays a floating-rate coupon, subject to the rule that if Libor exceeds a particular value, such as 10%, then that value will be used instead. This instrument is really a floater minus an option on each Libor fixing. This series of options is known as a *cap*, and each of the little options is known as a *caplet*. Some FRNs have an embedded *floor*, so if Libor drops below the floor then the floor is used instead. This would be an FRN plus a floor (itself composed of a series of *floorlets*).

In the US most mortgages are at a fixed rate, but they may be repaid early. Consider the position of a homeowner who has bought a house, using money borrowed against an 8% 30-year mortgage. If mortgage rates rise, the homeowner does nothing. But if they fall, the homeowner can repay this mortgage, and refinance (refi) at the new lower rate. It is common practice in US financial markets to take a few thousand mortgages and combine their cashflows into a bond. The holder of the bond receives the appropriate share of the payments made by the home-owners, less a management fee. Such a *mortgage-backed security* (MBS) is not a fixed-rate bond, because if interest rates fall then the bond is repaid soon. The holder of the bond has, in effect, sold an option to the homeowner. Pricing the option embedded in mortgages is complicated.

Implied volatility

We have already discussed at length the concept of the yield of a bond. This can be thought of as a breakeven funding rate; if an investor's cost of borrowing is no more expensive than a bond's yield, then ownership of the bond will be profitable. But the fund-ing rate will vary over the life of the bond, so the yield of the bond represents a breakeven average cost of funding.

There is a similar concept for options. Options are worth owning if the price of the underlying asset is volatile. An option's price implies a breakeven amount of volatility; the breakeven amount of volatility is called *implied volatility*.

Let us compare two examples. If a bond has a yield of 5%, that means the breakeven constant borrowing rate for the lifetime of the bond is 5%. If an option has an implied volatility of 17%, then the price of the underlying needs to vary by ±17% each year to justify the option price.

So, if a gold future is quoted at $250 and the price of a 1-year option is such that implied volatility is about 17%, then the market is expecting a move of about ±$42.50 in the price of that future over the next year. Note, however, that implied volatilities do not compound in the same manner as interest rates.[†]

[†] Volatilities scale proportionately to the square root of time, so the implied standard deviation of the distribution of the logarithm of the expiry price of the underlying is volatility $\times \sqrt{\text{time}}$. For example, if a 6-month option on an asset costing £10 has an implied volatility of 17%, the market is expecting a move in the price between now and expiry of about £10 $\times$ 17% $\times \sqrt{1/2} \approx \pm£1.20$.

Options on bonds are more confusing, as the implied volatility can be quoted as if the price of the bond were the underlying, or as if the yield of the bond were the underlying.

Summary

- Options allow market users to keep the upside while only risking the cost of the option.
- A call option gives the right to buy an underlying asset, and a put option gives the right to sell.
- Implied volatility measures the breakeven volatility of the price of the underlying.
- Higher implied volatility implies a higher option price.
- Options are often traded in combinations and they can be embedded in other financial instruments.

Chapter 6

Foreign exchange

The basic rationale

Countries trade with each other. The British sell whisky and gin to the Japanese; the Japanese sell electronic goods to the British; both sell to the Americans and buy Hollywood films from them. All three sell tourism to each other.

Each of these transactions necessitates a foreign exchange (FX) market. For instance, a gin importer in America will wish to buy sterling and sell dollars. The importer's bank may well provide this service. But selling sterling to the importer will take the bank short of sterling, and if the bank does not want to keep the short-GBP and long-USD position that it has acquired, it will buy sterling from another bank. In this way the position is passed from one hand to the next, until it reaches someone willing to hold it—at least temporarily.

Trade-related flows are important to the foreign exchange market, but more important are *capital* flows, which are investment-related flows. The most visible of these are takeovers. If an American company is buying a British company for £10 billion and is paying for it in cash rather than shares, then that American company may well be selling $15 billion to buy £10 billion (using a GBP/USD exchange rate of 1.50). These takeover- and investment-related flows are some of the most important drivers of the price action in FX markets.

Size and conventions

The FX market is huge. It is possible to trade significant fractions of a billion dollars in the largest currency pairs, EUR/USD and USD/JPY, while moving the price less than one-tenth of a percent. The Bank for International Settlements estimates that the typical daily turnover is of value $1.5 trillion. The FX market is fast-moving. By convention, a price made by telephone is *good* for two seconds: that is how long the other side has to accept. However, trading is increasingly electronic.

Unless otherwise agreed, foreign exchange transactions are T+2. That is, if a trade is agreed on a Monday, the money changes hands on the Wednesday. The one exception is the USD/CAD rate, which is T+1. For all FX rates, there are rules that determine how far forward the default settlement date is moved if public holidays intervene.

Forwards

There is also a large and active market in foreign exchange for a non-standard settlement date. Any settlement date beyond the conventional T+2 is described as *forward*. In principle, pricing of forward FX is simple.

We take an example, in which we want to know the 1-year forward price of USD/JPY. Let us assume that *spot* USD/JPY (i.e. for T+2 delivery) is at 110, that 1-year JPY Libor is 0.50%, and that 1-year USD Libor is 7%. What is the price of USD/JPY for delivery 1 year after spot delivery (i.e. in 1 year and 2 days)?

We know three relationships. The first is the 1-year dollar interest rate, which connects spot dollars to forward dollars:

$$1 \text{ USD}_{spot} = 1.07 \text{ USD}_{spot+1Y}$$

The second is the spot FX rate, which connects spot dollars to spot yen:

$$1 \text{ USD}_{spot} = 110 \text{ JPY}_{spot}$$

The third is the 1-year yen interest rate, which connects spot yen to forward yen:

$$1 \text{ JPY}_{spot} = 1.005 \text{ JPY}_{spot+1Y}$$

From these it can be deduced that

$$1 \text{ USD}_{spot+1Y} = \frac{110 \times 1.005}{1.07} \text{ JPY}_{spot+1Y}$$

$$\approx 103.32 \text{ JPY}_{spot+1Y}$$

So 1 year forward a US dollar costs ¥103.32, some ¥6.68 cheaper than for spot settlement. The *1-year FX points* are therefore −668. However, because FX market participants know the sign of the points for any given currency pair, a minus sign is usually omitted: the 1-year USD/JPY points would be quoted as 668.

(This calculation has been slightly simplified by the omission of several minor details.)

Shake the dice

Financial markets may appear to be a casino, but actually they serve a purpose, an important purpose, and in general they are well designed to serve that purpose. This is true of foreign exchange and forwards and *vanilla options*, all of which have genuine uses. They are needed by importers and exporters of real goods and services, and also by investors and borrowers (exporters and importers of capital).

However, some of the *exotic options* that are traded in the FX market have fewer obvious uses. To this author they appear to be purely speculative and rarely related to any genuine real-world economic activity. Nonetheless, they are an important part of the foreign exchange market, and hence they require some explanation.

It is easiest to start with an example. Imagine that the USD/JPY exchange rate is currently 108.50. Consider a vanilla USD call JPY put, struck at ¥109. This gives the holder the right to buy some number of US dollars for a cost of ¥109 each, and at expiry this option is therefore worth ¥1 for each ¥1 the dollar is above ¥109. Now add an extra clause: if the USD/JPY exchange rate touches ¥111, however briefly, then the option is cancelled. The option's payoff at expiry will be as in the diagram, with a peak payoff of just under ¥2 if the exchange rate is almost at ¥111 but without having actually reached it.

Expiry value of a ¥109 USD call JPY put, with a ¥111 knockout

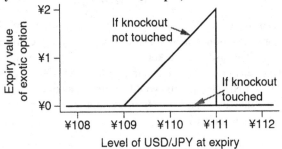

Let us add an extra clause: assume that the above option has 1 month to expiry, and add an extra knockout at ¥108, but this ¥108 knockout applies only for the first week. So if USD/JPY touches 108 in the first week, or touches 111 at any time during the option's 1-month life, then the option disappears; otherwise it is a vanilla 109 call.

It is hard to imagine that there is a genuine risk hedged by this structure. Indeed, except in rare cases, it appears to be purely a gambling instrument. But it is a gambling instrument with interesting consequences. Consider the position of an investment bank which sold one almost a month ago; it is now lunchtime on expiry day, the option expires at 3 pm, and USD/JPY is 110.70. It would be very tempting to try to trigger the knockout by pushing USD/JPY to 111.01. So the investment bank sells lots of yen for dollars to push the price of a dollar higher, and once 111.01 has been reached, these dollars are sold and the price quickly collapses back.

And whoever bought the option is in the reverse position, and may be willing to defend the knockout by selling lots of dollars just under ¥111. A battle can develop, and whichever party is the larger or more determined will win. And while this battle is in play, the price action in USD/JPY will have little connection to news about the two economies, business flows or trade flows. Exotic options are therefore important because of the short-term distorting effect that they sometimes have on the underlying FX rates.

Summary

- Foreign exchange markets allow importers and exporters to trade, and facilitate cross-border investments and takeovers.
- Forward FX prices are calculated using the interest rate differential between the two currencies.
- Options on FX are actively traded.
- Exotic options, with barriers or knockouts, sometimes drive the prices of the underlying currencies.

Chapter 7

Players

We have now discussed the basic tools of trading the cost of money: the money market, bonds, futures, swaps, options and foreign exchange. Who uses them, why, and what for? There are several different types of player, some borrowers and some lenders, each of whom has different motivations and constraints.

Governments

Governments borrow money by issuing bonds. In general, governments issue fixed-rate debt in their domestic currency, with maturities up to about 30 years. Governments are not very price-sensitive in their issuance: the amounts that they issue are generally determined by their need for cash, not by the prevailing yields.

Because government bonds are so important to investors, there are several government bond indices. These are the bond equivalents of the S&P 500 or the FTSE 100. Such an index shows the combined return from capital gains and coupons, known as the *total return*, of a particular bond portfolio. Portfolios from which indices are made usually consist of all bonds of a certain type. These are usually divided into sub-indices by currency, issuer and maturity range.

Pseudo-government issuers

Entities other than governments also issue bonds. Some of these entities are of such impeccable credit that, for investment purposes, their debt is treated as a pseudo-government debt.

In the US the most important such entities are the *agencies*, more formally known as the Government-Sponsored Enterprises (GSEs). Many of these agencies were formed during the recession of the 1930s, and lend money to homeowners, either directly or indirectly. Among the largest agencies are Fannie Mae, Freddie Mac and Ginnie Mae. They fund these loans by selling debt in the capital markets. This debt is not explicitly guaranteed by the government. However, in the markets it is widely believed that the US government would not allow any of these GSEs to fail; they are said to be *implicitly guaranteed.*

Debt is also issued by various supranational entities, such as the World Bank and the EIB. Many supranational issuers have a *funding target*, and they borrow when they can borrow cheaper than the target. For example, one of the large supranationals currently has a target of 3-month USD Libor – 35bp. This funding target drives its issuance behaviour; it is willing to issue debt in any currency and in any form, if that debt can be swapped backed into floating-rate dollars, with an all-in funding cost of no more than 35bp below USD Libor.

One of the largest of the supranational borrowers is the World Bank, which has issued large quantities of long-dated fixed-coupon debt in sterling. Simultaneously with issuing such a security, the World Bank transacts a swap, receiving fixed-coupon sterling versus paying floating-rate dollars, a type of cross-currency swap discussed in more detail in Chapter 10. This converts the World Bank's fixed-rate sterling liability into a floating-rate dollar liability. The swapped issuance means that the supranationals are large and important participants in the swap market.

Non-financial corporations

Corporations both borrow and lend money. In their capacity as borrowers they issue tradable debt in the full range of maturities, and in fixed- and floating-rate forms.

Entities such as utilities (water, gas and electricity companies) tend to issue long-dated fixed-coupon debt. The income of such a utility is fairly steady, and certainly does not vary with short-term interest rates. Therefore their liabilities are a better match for their income if they are in fixed- rather than floating-rate form.

Other corporations may prefer floating-rate debt. Typically this debt will be in one of the currencies in which the corporation earns its profits, or alternatively the debt will be swapped into such a currency. Large corporations actively manage a liability portfolio across different currencies and maturities.

Corporations sometimes issue asset-backed securities (ABS). This is tradable debt that is backed by some asset, much like a mortgage. Such assets might include its inventories of raw materials or finished goods, or perhaps debts owed to the company by its customers. If the company should default, the bondholders have first claim on the asset securing the bond.

Corporations also act as investors. Many companies maintain a cash pile, particularly if planning a takeover. This cash may well be invested in short-dated government bonds.

Exporters, importers and those mounting takeovers in different currencies—all are important players in the foreign exchange market.

Pension funds

As governments across the world reduce the generosity of state pensions, individuals increasingly need to save for their retirement. In many jurisdictions, saving money in a pension fund offers significant tax advantages over saving in any other manner. And hence many people make regular or occasional payments into a pension fund.

These streams of payments into pension funds make pension funds massive long-term investors in financial markets. They dominate both equity and bond markets, and tend to accumulate long-dated fixed-coupon bonds, whether issued by governments or by corporations.

A typical pension fund is much too large to be managed by a single individual. Instead there is a hierarchy of investment. At the top level, a committee will decide on the division between equities, fixed income (bonds), cash, property, and other investment classes. Advice from the pension fund's actuary will have a great influence on this split. If the fund is young, with most of its beneficiaries in their twenties or thirties, the pension fund will give a greater weighting to equities. If the fund is mature, with many beneficiaries approaching pensionable age or already drawing pensions, then a higher proportion of its assets will be in fixed income. Whatever the split, instructions cascade down to the portfolio managers. Typically, these instructions take the form of an index; the manager is instructed to manage an amount of money in such manner as to outperform a certain index.

And hence much invested money is being managed with the intention of outperforming an index, or at least not underperforming it by much. Indexed investors therefore tend to own the bonds of which the target index is composed. This means that such investors buy bonds as they enter the index, and sell them as they leave. Further, coupons are reinvested across the whole index, i.e. in each of the bonds in the index.

In US dollars there are several important bond indices. These include the *Lehman Aggregate*, which contains Treasuries, bonds issued by the GSEs and private-sector corporations and mortgage-backed securities; the *Salomon BIG*, consisting of much the same securities; and the *Lehman Treasury Index*, containing just the US Treasuries. In the eurozone the most important is the *J. P. Morgan Euro Index*, consisting of all the liquid fixed-coupon eurozone government debt with over 1 year to maturity, and in sterling the *Financial Times Actuaries 15+ Gilt Index*, consisting of all conventional gilts with over 15 years to maturity. Many Japanese investors track the *Nomura Bond Index*, which is composed of JGBs and non-government yen bonds with a credit rating of at least single-A.

Insurers

Insurers engage in two main activities. First, insurers sell policies on cars, houses, and such like. The client pays a premium, and if the client's car crashes or their house is burgled, the insurer pays. At the start the insurer receives the premium, and hence has money to invest. By and large, the insurer can invest in any investments that it thinks will perform well. However, the insurer doesn't have an absolutely free hand; regulators do insist that its portfolio of investments must be appropriately prudent.

Second, insurers sell annuities. An annuity is a sum of money paid at regular intervals. A *life annuity* will pay this sum for the rest of the beneficiary's life. This can be thought of as insurance against living too long: those that die early do not extract the full benefit of their annuity; those that live long are in effect subsidised by those that don't.

The method by which annuities are usually purchased is driven by local law, especially tax laws. In some jurisdictions annuities are purchased through a savings plan; money is paid into the plan before retirement. In other jurisdictions, annuities interact with pension law. In these countries, pension funds pay their value as a lump sum on retirement, but the retiree is obliged to use this sum to purchase an annuity. The life annuity provides a monthly payment that may be a fixed sum or a sum linked to inflation. In either case the natural hedge for these annuities is to own bonds, and an insurer's life portfolio will typically be invested mostly in fixed income, including both government and quality-credit non-government bonds. Life insurance businesses are also regulated, but the details of the regulation vary greatly from jurisdiction to jurisdiction.

Some insurers and pension funds have created in-house investment managers, managing not only their own money but also that of external clients. The external clients typically specify some constraints on how the money is invested. Again, the method used is *indexing*; the client tells the fund manager that the fund is to outperform an index. A fund that is tracking an index will typically own a mix of assets very similar to those in the index.

Mutual funds

Mutual funds are investment vehicles that pool the savings of private individuals. In most countries mutual funds are more flexible than a pension fund, but do not have its tax advantages.

Mutual funds come in two types. Each investor in an *open-ended* mutual fund is deemed to own a proportionate share of the assets. Units are purchased or redeemed at a price equal to the value of the share of the assets. There is an annual management fee, and perhaps also a fee on purchase or redemption.

A *closed-end* mutual fund is a company that accepts money when it starts in business. Some pay dividends, some have a predetermined winding-up date. A closed-end fund is traded on a stock exchange, and the price at which it trades can be greater or less than the value of its assets.

So an open-ended fund is of variable size, but the value of a unit always equals the value of the underlying assets. In contrast, a closed-end fund is of fixed size, which allows the managers to invest in illiquid assets, or in assets that are difficult to trade.

There are mutual funds which invest in equities, some which invest in property, and some in bonds. Of the bond mutual funds, some passively track a government bond index, others are more actively managed and allowed to invest in non-government bonds. Bond mutual funds are particularly important in the US, Italy, Belgium and Luxembourg.

Hedge funds

Hedge funds accept risk capital from a small number of rich individuals and other institutions, and trade this aggressively in the markets. Hedge funds are usually leveraged. That is, a hedge fund may take positions that are many times larger than its capital, using repo to borrow the extra. Hedge funds are also willing to sell assets that they don't own, using repo to borrow those assets.

Some hedge funds are *macro*, in that they trade the state of the world economy. They may buy or sell currencies, stock markets and bonds, or futures on any of these, as well as commodities such as oil, precious metals and base metals. Others are *micro*, in that they trade relative value between similar instruments. They might buy one bond and sell another bond of similar maturity, or they might trade bonds against swaps, or one option against a different option. Between them, hedge funds are willing to execute any trade that they believe will be profitable.

Commercial banks

Banks are varied and complicated players in financial markets. Their classic business is taking deposits from the public and making loans, either secured in the form of mortgages or unsecured in the form of overdrafts for individuals and businesses.

The deposits and the loans are mismatched. A bank's borrowing is mostly short-term; it pays a floating interest rate, and depositors can withdraw their money at little or no notice. The lending is long-term, in that the bank cannot demand instant repayment. So, to allow depositors to make withdrawals, banks need to keep some money in a safe and readily realisable form, such as government bonds or other easily sold securities.

Where does this money, this *capital*, come from? Clearly, it can't come from another deposit, as that depositor may suddenly withdraw the money. The capital needs to be long-term. Also, the source of the capital must be *junior* to the depositors; if the bank becomes insolvent, the depositors must be paid in full before the provider of this capital gets anything.

Capital can come from a number of sources. Capital can be in the form of *retained profits* that have not been paid out to the shareholders in the form of dividends. Capital can come more immediately from shareholders, as the proceeds of the company issuing new shares, a *rights issue*. Or banks can borrow capital, but this must be a long-term borrowing, and the debt must be junior to the depositors in the event of insolvency. Very junior debt is said to be *subordinated*; non-subordinated debt is often called *senior debt*.

Bank regulators determine the meanings of such terms such as 'junior' and 'long-term'. The rules are guided by the Basel Accord of 1988; a revision to this accord is currently being finalised. The Basel Accord is an agreement between bank regulators that partly harmonises the regulation of bank capital across many countries. Nonetheless, the details of the regulations differ from one jurisdiction to another, and they change from time to time within jurisdictions.

So banks need to raise capital by issuing junior debt in a form that satisfies bank regulators. The banks also want this debt to have the best possible tax status. This interaction between bank regulation, tax law, and the bank's own interest is often resolved in complicated ways. As an example, let us now look at the *step-up perpetual*.

In a number of jurisdictions, bank regulations greatly favour the issuance of perpetual debt. The debt has no final maturity date; instead, coupons are paid forever. However, investors believe that such debt entails a huge credit risk, and so they demand that the yield be far above that of the long-dated government bond. What the issuing bank wants is debt that looks like a perpetual to the regulator but like finite-maturity debt to the investor.

The solution is called a step-up perpetual. For example, this might be a floating-rate bond that pays a floating-rate coupon of Libor + 1%. This bond is *callable* after 15 years; that is, the issuer has the option to call the bond. If it is called then it is redeemed at

100, just as if it had an original maturity of 15 years. But if the issuer does not exercise this call option, the bond prospectus specifies that the coupon automatically steps up to Libor + 5%.

So if the issuer does not call the bond, the penalty is expensive; in this example it is an extra 4% per year. Because of this penalty, the bank has an incentive to call the bond, and so the investors believe it will be called. The investors believe that, for practical purposes, the bond will have a finite maturity, and so the credit spread, the difference in yield between this and a government bond, can be narrower than for a perpetual. This cheapens the issuer's cost of funding.

Other complications can intrude. For tax reasons, in some jurisdictions the bond is actually issued by a separate company known as a *special purpose vehicle* (SPV), and that company, or just the bond, is guaranteed by the bank. Also note that regulations in some countries impose a minimum time to step up, and a maximum amount that the coupon may step up.

To summarise, there is a large market in bank capital securities. This market is driven by the details of bank regulations and tax codes, and within these, the issuers trying to minimise the cost of funding. The interaction between these rules and incentives creates complicated securities.

Mortgage lenders

Many financial institutions lend money to homeowners, and this lending is often in the form of a mortgage. A mortgage can be thought of as a form of repo; a bank lends money to a homeowner and improves the credit of the loan by taking the deeds of the property or by having some right over it. Some mortgages are floating-rate, in that the lender changes the interest rate frequently to reflect changes in the central bank's official interest rate. In other countries the mortgage rate is fixed, typically for 2 to 5 years in the UK, and for up to 30 years in the US and in much of continental Europe.

This mismatch means that mortgage lenders are taking substantial interest-rate risk. If short-term interest rates were to rise, these institutions would have to pay more to their depositors, but they would continue to receive the old low payments from their mortgage assets. It used to be that this risk went unhedged. In the US in the 1980s, when short-term interest rose hugely, this mismatch drove many thrifts, similar to UK building societies, into insolvency. Cleaning up the mess cost the US taxpayer many tens of billions of dollars. Nowadays, mortgage lenders in all the main currencies are careful to measure and hedge their interest-rate risk. This makes them active participants in interest-rate futures, swaps and government bonds.

Central banks

We have already described how governments borrow money, typically in their own currency. But governments also keep a supply of money for use in emergencies. In an emergency the domestic currency might devalue by a large factor, particularly if the country is perceived to be losing a major war. And hence governments keep reserves, usually in gold, dollars and in other foreign currencies. In a war or other emergency it is believed that these could be used to buy essentials, such as food, oil and weapons. For example, at the start of 2000, Japan's foreign exchange reserves totalled about \$220 billion and the UK's about \$38 billion.

In most countries the management of foreign exchange reserves is done by the central bank. Central banks avoid owning their foreign exchange reserves in the form of banknotes, because banknotes pay no interest. Instead, governments typically invest their foreign exchange reserves in low-risk assets, especially short-dated government debt. While most central banks hold the bulk of their reserves in dollars and gold, quantities are also held, in decreasing order, in euros, yen, and sterling.

Private investors

In most countries, institutional players dominate financial markets. These institutions aggregate the investments or the liabilities of many private individuals, and invest or borrow on their behalf. We have seen this in the form of pension funds (long-term saving), life insurance (a different form of long-term saving), mortgage lenders who borrow from the financial markets, and governments and central banks acting on behalf of taxpayers.

However, private investors sometimes act in the financial markets themselves, usually as investors. The investment behaviour of individuals is typically strongly influenced by tax law, and hence it differs greatly from one jurisdiction to another. In bond markets, private investors have been important in Italy, Belgium and Austria. But currently, in most bond markets, and especially in those of the US, UK and Germany, the price action is driven almost entirely by institutional players.

Summary

- The government is usually the most important issuer of bonds in its domestic currency.
- Various supranational entities and government-guaranteed entities are also prolific issuers, but their style of issuance also makes them active in the swap market.
- Non-financial corporations are both borrowers and lenders.
- Pension funds and insurers are the longest-term investors. Much money in their care is invested so as to match an index, which makes the indices important to financial markets.
- Commercial banks raise capital in the debt market. The form that this takes can be a complicated compromise between the requirements of the bank regulators, the tax laws, and investors' preferences.

- Central banks are active in their domestic money market. They also manage foreign exchange reserves, which tend to be invested in short-dated low-risk assets, mostly in dollars.
- The investment behaviour of private investors is highly tax sensitive.

Chapter 8

People

Introduction

Financial markets employ many people. For a typical investment bank, staff remuneration amounts to over half of all costs. Some of the remainder will be on services rendered by other companies, which also employ people. As well as being a bank's main expense, people are its main asset. And people can be difficult to manage, particularly during a merger or takeover, when the best staff may not want to risk staying—a bank's main asset can walk out of the door.

As in any business, in investment banking there are no hard and fast boundaries between what various people do. However, this chapter describes several of the distinct roles on a trading floor.

Proprietary traders

Proprietary traders 'prop traders' use their employer's money to make more money. The dictionary defines *proprietary* as 'held as property', and prop traders speculate with the bank's property, that is, with the bank's money. Like hedge funds, some proprietary traders are *macro*, trading the state of the world economy, and others are *micro*, trading relative value within an asset class. Some banks even structure their prop trading desk as an internal hedge fund.

Whatever the type of trading, prop traders' profit and loss (P&L) is carefully measured, as is the risk that is being taken. All traders, including prop traders, have risk limits. The riskiness of their position is estimated at least daily, and it must not exceed management guidelines. If a trader buys something, the daily P&L account will make proper allowance for the cost of borrowing the money needed to do this. Equally, if the trader sells something, the P&L account will allow for the cost of borrowing the asset.

At the very extreme, the best prop traders might make profits each year of the order of several hundred million dollars. Prop traders' pay is not a fixed percentage, and will typically depend on the steadiness of the profits and the risks taken. However, 8% to 15% is not unusual. Many of the wealthiest people in finance are, or were, prop traders.

An ambitious reader should note that most banks would not consider employing someone as a prop trader without at least five years of market experience. Nonetheless, the reader may be interested in some clues as to how to do the job well.

A good prop trader must always be disciplined when faced with a losing position. It might be that the reduced price of acquiring the trade means that it is now even better value, and hence the trade should be increased in size. Alternatively, it might be that the adverse price action shows that the original reasoning was flawed, and that the position should now be closed. The trader should not become 'married to the position'; the belief about markets should determine the trade, the trade must not determine the belief. The best test that can be applied is to ask, 'If I did not have this position, would I now choose to acquire it?' If the answer is no, take losses and be glad that they aren't larger. Don't let pride and egoism obstruct clear thinking; a trader who refuses to take any loss may end up having to take a far larger loss.

A similar but less stressful question occurs with winning positions. Perhaps profits should be taken, or perhaps the move in the price somehow shows that the original reasoning was right, and therefore that the risk should be increased. In either case, reason it out from the beginning. A good prop trader makes a profit in three out of five trades, and the average size of any profit is at least twice the average size of any loss. Losses are acceptable but they should be small.

In some investment banks, prop traders take huge positions. Sometimes these positions can be of similar size to the market; an easy way to ensure that the price of a bond goes up is to buy all of it. Prop traders should be certain that any such positions satisfy the house position limits, the exchange rules, and any relevant laws.

Market makers

Market makers quote prices to clients. They are often asked to quote two prices: a buying and a selling, or a lending and a borrowing. So a market maker in Swiss franc deposits will quote a rate at which money will be lent, and a slightly lower rate at which deposits will be accepted. A market maker in a government bond will quote a *bid* price, at which the market maker is willing to buy, and a slightly higher *offer* price at which the market maker is willing to sell. The market maker's job is to capture this bid-offer spread while hedging out the residual risk as cheaply as possible.

Market makers usually quote the *little digits*. If a bond's price is somewhere near 101.75, and a market maker quotes 'seventy-four seventy-seven', usually written 74/77, that means the market maker is willing to pay 101.74 for 100 nominal of the bond, and would accept 101.77. If the market maker were less keen to buy and more keen to sell, the price might have been 73/76.

Market makers inevitably acquire *cross books*, that is, a collection of almost offsetting positions. For example, if a market maker sells some 4-year bonds to a client and then some 6-years, the cheapest hedge to execute may be to buy some 5-years. This can be thought of as a hedge. Alternatively, it can be thought of as a trade, long 5s against 4s and 6s, a position from which the market maker hopes to make a profit. Obviously, the aim is to ensure that the long positions are of relatively cheap bonds, and the short positions are of relatively expensive bonds.

Depending on which book is being traded, a market maker should have an annual profit of a few million dollars to a few dozen million. As with prop traders, there is no set percentage; the actual pay depends on the steadiness of the profits, the risks taken and the extent to which clients are kept happy. But, having said that, 6% to 10% is not unusual.

The same trading advice applies to market makers as to proprietary traders, with one additional point. Most banks want to record a closing price of the instruments that they trade. In some cases, particularly futures, closing prices are published by an exchange. But a bank needs to record its own closing prices in the likes of bonds and swaps. The person who best knows the true market price is generally the market maker, and so the market maker chooses the closing prices. However, banks do have internal controls that verify whether these closes make sense; claiming fictitious profits is a serious offence.

Even so, there is a little room for manoeuvre within the bid-offer spread, especially in those instruments that trade infrequently. This can give rise to a temptation to 'adjust' profits; putting a little away into reserves on winning days, and taking it out again on losing days. However, such behaviour reduces trading discipline, and also makes it far harder for researchers to use historic prices to find profitable trades.

Brokers

Brokers do not trade on their own account; they facilitate trading by others and they are paid a commission. Some brokers serve a retail market. They provide the general public with access to the equity, bond and futures markets, allowing them to trade on their own account. This may be done face-to-face, in a bank branch, by phone or over the internet.

Other brokers serve the professional market. Consider the position of a dealer who owns a particular bond, and would like to reduce the size of the position. The trader does not want to contact the competition directly, for fear they would mark down the price once they knew there was a large seller. A broker intermediates. A good broker knows who might be a buyer to match a seller and the true market price of the instrument. If the trade is done, the broker takes a commission.

Some brokers, particularly those in the swap market, can become wealthy. Many others make a very reasonable living.

Salespeople

Salespeople talk to clients. Ultimately, financial markets exist to satisfy the needs of end-users, matching borrowers with investors. Salespeople, sometimes known as *marketers*, talk to these end-users.

The job of salespeople is to bring in the business of these end-users. If an investor wants to buy or sell, that enquiry is routed through a salesperson. Sales should also be able to target business: if the market-making desk is long a particular asset, a salesperson's job is to find a long-term home for it; if the desk is short, to find a seller. Salespeople also provide intelligence about what clients are doing and what they might be about to do. All of this requires that salespeople know their clients, what they own and what types of trade they might be willing to do; the salespeople communicate this information to the market makers.

From the client's viewpoint, salespeople are the gateway to the services provided by an investment bank. These include the ability to deal in a wide range of financial markets, research about those markets, access to the researchers, historic data and the passwords to the models and reports published on the web. The best sales-people can be paid as much as the best market makers.

Researchers

Most banks have some form of research department, employing many different types of analyst. Some will be macroeconomists, forecasting inflation, the growth of the economy, and most importantly, the likely response of the central bank. Others will be credit analysts, commenting on the relative creditworthiness of different issuers or different bonds. There will also be more mathematical researchers, building and testing various models. In the equity market, some analysts become famous and as well paid as the best market makers, but this is rare in fixed income.

Back office and middle office

So, a trade has been agreed. The bank sells and the client buys a bond. Money needs to change hands, and the bond needs to be transferred. Swap transactions are more complicated, entailing periodic payments between the parties for a number of years. The back office deals with this work. When a trade is done, the two parties' back offices exchange confirmations and then exchange payments and securities. Most organisations now have a middle office. Middle-office staff tend to be seated on the trading floor, and liaise as necessary between back office, traders and sales staff to resolve settlement errors.

Investment bankers

Assume that a company which makes bolts wishes to take over a company which makes nuts. The bolt-making company knows everything there is to know about bolts, but its expertise does not include financial markets. It will want advice and assistance. This will cover the takeover itself, and also related matters such as raising the money and dealing with tax and antitrust authorities.

Banks have departments that can give this advice and assistance; their names typically include the phrase 'investment banking' or 'mergers and acquisitions'. Advice is given in confidence, and the advisors are 'behind a Chinese wall'. Employees on the *inside* of the Chinese wall sit on a separate floor or even in a separate building to those on the *public* side. A trader, on the public side of the wall, is not given any advance notice of the deal. Investment banking departments make their money by charging fees for their services.

Summary

- Proprietary traders speculate with the bank's money.
- Market makers provide liquidity for clients, with the intention of capturing the bid-offer spread.
- Salespeople talk to clients to direct trades to the market makers and to gather information.
- Researchers provide information and analysis to traders, salespeople and clients.
- Back and middle offices arrange for confirmations to be exchanged with counterparties, and then ensure that all trades settle correctly.
- Investment bankers provide confidential advice to clients. Because the advice is confidential, they work behind a Chinese wall.

Chapter 9

Price action

Why do prices move?

Prices are made by buyers and sellers. There are no mysterious forces that link the economy or a measure of 'fair value' to price action; prices rise only because of buyers, and they fall only because of sellers.

Let us make this more concrete with an example. It happens to use a particular futures contract but the meaning is general. Futures contracts are generally traded electronically. Bids (to buy) and offers (to sell) are entered into a trade matching system: those that can be filled are filled, those that can't be filled wait in a *stack*. The example shows the state of the stack for the Mar2001 sterling interest-rate future (listed on LIFFE with code L H1) as of 14:15 on Wednesday 11 October 2000.

The stack has two sides, bids and offers. Currently the best bid is 93.73, and this price is bid for 1655 contracts. The next best bid is 93.72, for 1544 contracts. The best offer is 0.01 higher than the best bid, at 93.74, and 427 contracts are offered at this price.

Let us imagine that a trader needs to buy some of these contracts. As a first case, assume that the trader wants some of

| | L H1 | |
| | 14:15 Wed 11 Oct 00 | |
Bid size	Price	Offer size
	94.11	79
	93.81	10
	93.78	20
	93.77	100
	93.76	822
	93.75	667
	93.74	427
1655	93.73	
1544	93.72	
495	93.71	
850	93.70	
151	93.69	
101	93.68	
50	93.67	
11	93.65	

these contracts, but not urgently enough that the trader is willing to pay 93.74 for them. The trader may well 'join the bid at 73'. Note that the '93.' goes unstated, just the decimals are spoken. If the trader bid for 200 contracts, the stack would then show 73 bid for 1655 + 200 = 1855 contracts.

Alternatively, perhaps the trader needs these 200 contracts urgently enough to pay 74 for them. The disadvantage of the higher price would be offset by the certainty of the trade. Bidding 73 would not guarantee getting anything; bidding 74 guarantees an immediate *fill*.

But what if the urgent need were for 1500 contracts? Our trader could then lift all those on offer at 74 (427 of them), and those on offer at 75 (667), and then another 406 of the contracts on offer at 76. All done, 1500 contracts would be bought for an average price of just under 75.

So in the first case, there might not be a trade at all. In the second case, 74 would trade. In the third case, 74 would trade, then 75, and then 76. The price action would reflect the desperation of the buyer.

Our keen buyer of 1500 contracts has other choices. A reasonable course would be to pay 74 for 300 contracts (leaving 127 on the offer at 74, so that it isn't too obvious there is a large buyer about) and then to bid 73 for 500 contracts. The bid for the remaining 700 contracts would be kept in hand and only entered into the system as the 73 bid started to be filled.

Our would-be buyer has more devious possibilities. Again, pay 74 for 300 contracts, leaving 127 on the offer at 74. Then offer several thousand contracts at 75, to make it appear that someone is a large seller just above the current price. This might encourage those currently offering the 667 contracts at 75 to improve their terms, and to offer them at 74, 0.01 cheaper. If they do, these contracts can be bought, and the offer at 75 cancelled.

Of course, this strategy isn't riskless—if someone else were to buy those contracts offered at 75, then they would have to be repurchased at a still higher price. A good trader has the ability to do one thing while appearing to do another; an even better trader has the ability to recognise when this is being attempted.

Necessity never made a good bargain

In the previous examples, the price action was driven by the urgency and desperation of the buyer. Of course, if it had been a seller in need of a large and quick deal, the price action would have been downwards rather than upwards, but the same principle would apply. Let us now imagine that everybody knows there is a desperate buyer. Offers at 74 or 75 would then be withdrawn, and replaced with offers of 76, 77 or 78: why sell low when one can be confident of selling high? So, prices are made by buyers and sellers, and prices will move against the more desperate. This is the essence of understanding and predicting price action: who needs to buy, who needs to sell, and how urgently. In the words of Benjamin Franklin, 'Necessity never made a good bargain'.

Stability and leverage

To illustrate price action, let us consider the market in a particular asset—it does not matter which. Let us imagine that there are some investors, each of whom has an estimate of the fair price of the asset. Each of these investors has some money kept as cash on deposit and some invested in the asset. If a new investor joins the crowd and buys, then the price will go up. The higher price will mean that some of the existing investors would believe it to be overpriced and would therefore sell. The price would settle at a new equilibrium, slightly higher than before.

Now imagine that there are also some leveraged players, such as hedge funds. These market participants have some money, but buy or sell in many times that size. So a leveraged player with $10 million might buy $100 million of the asset, borrowing the remaining $90 million using repo, or might sell $100 million of the asset, borrowing the asset using repo. Such trades are said to be *leveraged*; repo is being used in a manner analogous to a lever, so that $10 million of capital can be used to execute $100 million of trade. Let us also imagine that these market participants are leveraged between 5 and 20 times. Some are long, they own the asset; others are short, they have borrowed the asset and sold it, so in effect own a negative amount.

Let us imagine that, for some reason, the price jumps 5%. This might be because of some news relevant to the asset, or perhaps because a new investor is entering the market. The 5% jump means that anyone who was short is losing money. Someone who was leveraged 20 times has therefore lost all their risk capital: they had $10 million of money, had sold what was $200 million of the asset (for $200 million), but now require $210 million to buy it back. That investor's capital is exhausted, and the position must be closed.

Closing the position entails buying back the asset, increasing its price further. This may force other leveraged participants with short positions to close their positions, further driving up the price. The process ends only when all the leveraged shorts have bought back their positions.

The two cases are worth contrasting. When there is no leverage in the system, prices are stable, in that a higher price triggers selling and a lower price triggers buying. When there is enough leverage in the system then the reverse is true: higher prices trigger buying, to close losing positions; lower prices trigger selling.

Most of the time, most markets are stable. But the big moves in prices are often driven by a combination of surprise news and losing positions that must be unwound. The unwinding of the losing positions exacerbates the price action, triggering yet more *stop-losses*. There is a market saying that summarises this neatly: Prices move to inflict the maximum pain on those least able to take it.

Fixed-income prices

So far our discussion of price action has been very general, as applicable to Brent crude as to US Treasuries. However, we now focus on fixed-income prices in particular. There are many different factors that drive the price action in fixed-income markets, though at any one time only some of these will be active. The list below is therefore illustrative rather than exhaustive.

The first factor is the current level of official interest rates. If the central bank is lending money to the banking system at 3%, then the price at which the system is willing to lend money to the government for a year or so is likely to be between 2% and 4%. But were the central bank's interest rate nearer 20%, the government would probably have to pay a double-digit yield on its borrowings.

Information about the economy helps predict what the central bank will do next. For example, higher inflation is bad for fixed-income assets in one of two ways. It might be that the central bank is expected to react quickly to higher inflation, promptly raising interest rates. This would soon slow the economy, and later, after inflation had softened, rates could fall back. If this path of interest rates were to become expected, then the yield of short-dated bonds would rise more than the yield of long-dated bonds.

On the other hand, if it seems that the central bank is to ignore the higher inflation, then it depends on whether the rise in inflation is transient. If it is, then bonds need not fall. But if the inflation is not transient, then rates will still have to rise, although later and by more, which will particularly hurt long-dated bonds. So higher inflation typically hurts bonds, but the expected behaviour of the central bank determines in which maturity the yields increase the most.

Government statistical offices release other data. These include wage inflation, retail sales growth (in both price and volume), and gross domestic product (GDP), a measure of domestic output. Some business associations also publish surveys, having asked their members about their future investment intentions and their expectations of future order volumes and prices. All of this information contributes to the market's understanding of the economy, and no less importantly, to its understanding of the central bank's understanding.

These economic variables affect the buying and selling of bonds, but other influences can also be important. In most markets, pension funds and insurers are the dominant investors of long-dated bonds, and any change in the manner of their regulation can have knock-on effects. In some countries, especially the US and Denmark, there are complicated interactions between mortgage-backed securities and fixed-coupon government debt.

Supply of bonds is important but more confusing. When the economy is performing badly, governments' tax receipts tend to be lower than usual, and the larger than usual welfare payments ensure that expenditure is high. The government is therefore selling lots of bonds, and the presence of a large seller usually reduces the price. But the poor performance of the economy means that the central bank would have lowered (or would be about to lower) interest rates, and lower rates mean higher bond prices.

How do these forces balance out? In practice, low rates ensure that bonds and swaps have low yields. But the large supply of government bonds ensures that they yield only a little less than swaps. When the economy improves, and the supply of government bonds dries up, then government bonds will outperform swaps. When supply of government bonds is plentiful, they may well yield swaps – 25bp; when supply disappears they can yield as little as swaps – 125bp.

A stylised crash in fixed income

Chapter 3 gave a brief account of part of the 1994 fixed-income market crash. The following chart shows a stylised bond-market crash, based loosely on the 1994 crash in the US and UK, and the 1999 crash in the eurozone.

The story starts with line 1 in the chart overleaf, which shows the forward rates implied by market prices at time zero. Short-term rates were at 3% and the market was anticipating a gentle and slow rise in rates.

Line 2 is half a year later. There has been a surprise hike in the central bank's policy rate, followed by more hikes. Rates are now 4%, and clearly going up. The market is pricing for rates to continue increasing at the current pace for another year, then to continue rising but more slowly. The forward short-term rate $4\frac{1}{2}$ years out (i.e. 5 years after the start) is now priced at almost 7.5%. Six months previously, the same rate had been priced at just over 4%. During the previous six months there would have been panic selling on a number of occasions, as those who had borrowed money to buy bonds were forced to sell, cheapening them further.

Line 3 is 18 months after this, some two years after the start. The central bank has spent the time since line 2 raising rates, only an edge slower than then anticipated. However, rates are now

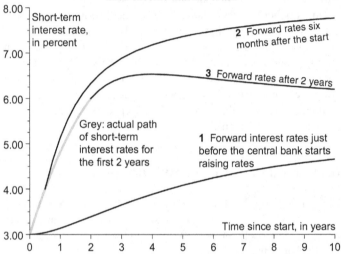

Development of forward rates during a stylised fixed-income market crash

believed to be near their peak. The market is unsure of the exact peak, but is pricing it at 6.5%, a little higher than the current level of 6%. However, once rates have reached this peak, the next move will be down, so the forward curve is slightly inverted beyond a few years out.

This sequence of events leaves many opportunities for winning and losing trades. But before explaining these trades, it will be helpful to discuss the relationship between the forward rates in the chart and *par rates* or bond yields.

Forwards, zeros and par yields

To see how interest rates vary with maturity, it is usual to plot a chart. But there are several different ways of expressing interest rates, and each gives a different picture. Three types of plot are common.

One can plot the forward rate, which is the interest rate for a short-term borrowing, starting at some time in the future. Sometimes the rate chosen is a generic *short-term rate* (as in the previous chart), but more commonly it is a 3-month, 6-month or 1-year rate. In this case the x-axis refers to the starting date of the short-term borrowing.

One can plot the *zero-coupon curve*. A zero-coupon yield is the cost of borrowing money from now until maturity, paying no coupons before maturity. This transaction involves only two cashflows: borrow money now, repay at maturity with compounded interest. In this case the x-axis refers to the maturity date of the borrowing. Borrowing in this fashion is equivalent to borrowing short-term, but also *locking in* the cost of each *rollover* of the short-term borrowing. Because of this equivalence, a 10-year zero-coupon yield equals the appropriately calculated average of the forward yields between now and 10 years out.

And one can plot the *par curve*. A par yield is the yield of a bond that does pay intervening coupons, whose size has been chosen to make the bond cost par (100). This transaction involves several cashflows: borrow money now, pay periodic coupons and at maturity also repay the principal. As in the zero-coupon case, the x-axis refers to the maturity date of the borrowing. So a par yield is just the yield of a bond costing 100.

The next chart shows this more clearly, using as its example the state of the yield curve 6 months into the stylised crash. The topmost of the three lines shows the forward rates, the market-implied cost of a short-term borrowing starting at some point in the future. So that this line is comparable with the next two, it is shown starting at time zero, and hence time zero on this line is 6 months into the crash.

Next are the zero-coupon rates. The 10-year zero-coupon rate is the average of the forward rates from time zero to that point. The averaging slows down the rate of increase from the starting level of 4%, so the zero-coupon curve is less steep than the forward

The relationship between the forward, zero and par yield curves

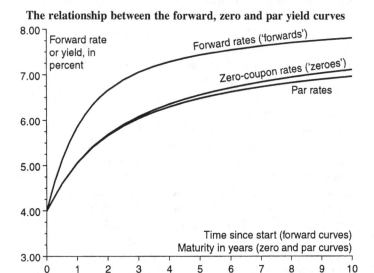

curve. Likewise, had the forward curve been *inverted*, starting high and ending low, then the zero-coupon curve would also have been inverted, but less so.

The par rates are the yields of bonds that cost par. In other words, for a given maturity, consider a bond paying a coupon of $y\%$, then choose y such that the bond costs 100. In doing this it is easiest to think about a strippable bond, so that each of the individual cashflows is traded and has its own yield. Then the yield of a par bond, which is the same as its coupon, is just a weighted average of the yields of its cashflows. But the cashflows, the strips, are themselves zero-coupon bonds maturing on the various payment dates. Therefore a par yield is an average of zero-coupon yields, so the par curve is even flatter than the zero-coupon curve. However, the largest payment is at the end, so the largest weighting in this average is on the final maturity payment, and hence the par curve is only slightly flatter than the zero-coupon curve.

As most investors trade coupon-paying bonds, it is natural to show the development of par rates during the crash, and there is a good reason why all the lines on this chart start at time zero.

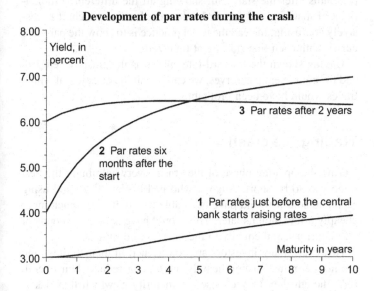

Development of par rates during the crash

The first chart of the crash showed market-implied forward rates at various times. These forward rates are directly comparable. For example, at the start of the crash, the market was expecting that 2 years later the short-term interest rate would be 3.39%. Six months into the crash, the market was expecting that the rate at time 2 years (i.e. 18 months later) would be 6.33%. Actually, 2 years after the start of the crash, rates were 6%. And hence the lines on the first chart are offset to display this direct comparability most effectively.

But par rates observed at different times are not directly

comparable. For example, at the start of the crash the 4-year par rate was 3.42%. With what rate can this be compared 6 months later? Certainly not the $3\frac{1}{2}$-year rate, as to do this would make no allowance for the level of interest rates during the first 6 months of the life of this 4-year par bond.

The correct course is, at the start, to calculate the $3\frac{1}{2}$-year rate 6 months forward, and compare this with the actual $3\frac{1}{2}$-year rate 6 months after the start. But showing all the different combinations of maturity and forward date would make the chart excessively confusing. Instead the usual practice is to show the par yield curve, with each line starting at time zero.

Having shown the forward-rate curves as the crash developed, and the equivalent par curves, we can revisit the question of which trades would have been profitable.

Trading the crash

During the opening phase of the crash, overwhelmingly the best trade was to be short. Anyone who had borrowed a bond using repo and sold it would have been able to buy it back much more cheaply a few months later. This would have applied to bonds of all maturities, and equally to the interest-rate futures.

However, many investors are constrained in their trading, and are not permitted to significantly increase or reduce their overall risk, though they may choose the maturity at which that risk is taken. Such an investor must, for example, decide whether to own 5 years, or to own some 2 years and some 10 years.

We return to the previous chart, showing par rates. In the opening move from line 1 to line 2, all the par rates rose. For very short-dated maturities, such as 2 years, they rose 2.5%; but from 5 to 10 years they rose in parallel by 3%. So 2s5s (the 5-year yield minus the 2-year yield) steepened, implying that 5s underperformed. In contrast, 5s10s moved in parallel. So a holder of 5s, obliged to maintain the market exposure, would have benefited by selling 5s into 2s and 10s.

In the second phase of the crash, the central bank's policy rate continued to rise. But it did not rise as fast as the forwards anticipated, and the long-dated forward yields actually fell. So the optimum strategy was to own bonds of the longest possible maturity. Long bonds rallied, and every part of the curve flattened.

So in summary our stylised crash moved the yield curves from being flat at a low level, to being steep and highly curved, and then to being flat at a high level. There were profitable opportunities for those able to trade the level of yields, or their steepness, or even just their curvature.

Market irrationality

Does the above example show that the market is irrational? Were there trades to do with guaranteed success? Well, yes and no. Clearly the market misjudged what was going to happen next. Before both of these crashes the market was pricing the possibility of a gentle rise in rates, albeit eventually. What actually happened was several rate rises, immediately.

But it might not have happened that way. For example, in mid-1992 the Bank of Japan (BoJ) cut its policy interest rate to 3.25%, after which the market was pricing that the BoJ's next move would be upwards. Actually it was a cut, to 2.5%, in early 1993. Again, after this the forward-rate curve was still pricing that the next move would be a hike. The actual outcome was lower rates, down to 1.75% in late 1993, then to 1% then 0.5%, then in several small quick steps to 0%. The zero interest rate policy (ZIRP) was maintained until August 2000, when the central bank's policy rate was hiked to a still tiny 0.25%; and in March 2001 this policy rate was again cut to 0%. Any trader positioned in the early 1990s for a Japanese bond-market crash would have made large losses.

Clearly it is important to anticipate the central bank's changes in short-term interest rates. Such anticipation requires an understanding of the economy and the central bank's understanding of the economy.

Summary

- Prices move because of buyers and sellers, and because of news that will affect buyers and sellers.
- In the absence of news, prices move against the most desperate, or against the most weakly held positions.
- Fixed-income markets care greatly about the central bank's policy rate, and about anything that may affect it in the future.
- Zero-coupon curves are flatter than forward-rate curves, and par curves are flatter still.
- Even in a bond-market crash, there are plenty of profitable opportunities: trading the level of yields, their steepness or even their curvature.

Part 2

More Detail

Chapter 10

Swaps revisited

Introduction

We saw in Chapter 4 that a swap transaction is effectively an exchange of deposits. In a vanilla interest-rate swap, one of these deposits will be at a fixed rate and one at a floating rate. In such a swap, the parties transfer only the difference in the fixed and floating interest payments. The small size of these transfers, typically less than 1% of the nominal size of the swap, ensures that the credit exposure in a swap is much less than in a loan of similar size. But there is some credit exposure in a swap, so we now discuss its extent and how it can be reduced. We then describe another form of swap, in which the exchanged deposits are in different currencies.

Credit risk in swaps

Let us revisit our earlier example of a swap, in which JPM receives 6% from CSFB for 10 years out of 15 Aug 07 in USD 100 million. Let us assume that this swap was agreed some time in early 2007, and that we are now in August 2007.

The agreed price of the swap is 6%. What if the market price, now in August 2007, for a 10-year USD swap is 7%? Well, JPM has agreed to receive 6% from CSFB. So CSFB could now agree to receive from JPM the current prevailing fixed rate of 7%; the two floating legs would cancel, and the only remaining obligation would be JPM's debt to CSFB of 1% per year for 10 years. Without worrying about the precise calculation, this payment stream is worth about $7.1 million.

This is the value of the swap. And if J. P. Morgan were to default at this time (August 2007), this is the sum of money that CSFB would have to write off. As it is, either counterparty can easily afford this sort of money, and a default by J. P. Morgan, a strongly rated money-centre bank, is extremely unlikely.

But a bank that is active in the swap market will typically have many thousands of live swap transactions at any one time, receiving and paying in different currencies from many different counterparties. With some of these counterparties the cumulative exposure can be large, equivalent to many tens or hundreds of millions of US dollars. Commonsense prudence, often reinforced by regulators' requirements, requires either that capital is set aside to protect against default, or that something else is done to reduce these credit risks.

Reducing the credit risk

So banks must either set aside capital, or protect themselves against default in some other way. Because setting aside capital is expensive, banks prefer to use credit improvement strategies. There are four such strategies: collateralisation, break clauses, recouponing and SwapClear.

Most swaps between professional counterparties (i.e. banks with active swap desks) are *collateralised*. When the swap is initially transacted, no collateral changes hands. But as market prices move, the swap will typically acquire a value. The *losing party* posts collateral with the *winning party*, and the amount of this collateral is frequently updated. So in our example, JPM would post $7.1 million of collateral with CSFB. If JPM were to default, CSFB could sell the collateral it holds; the proceeds of this sale would be equal to the value of the swap. Thus there are substantial collateral flows between the main swap dealers.

The second credit-improvement strategy entails the use of *break clauses*. If one party's credit has deteriorated below some specified level, then the break clauses allow the other party to terminate the swap, with its fair value being exchanged. The calculation of the fair value is done by a panel of five or so banks. Typically a swap might have a break after 10 years, and then further breaks every five years after that. The break dates must be agreed when the swap is initially transacted.

The third credit-improvement strategy entails *recouponing* swaps. We have described one swap between JPM and CSFB. These two counterparties might trade with each other in USD at least daily. So within a half-year or so there would be over a hundred outstanding swaps. To cut down the exposure, the two parties would then choose a portfolio of outstanding swaps that are far from par (i.e. have fixed legs or coupons substantially different from current market prices). The value of this portfolio of swaps would be agreed between the two parties, and this value paid by the losing party in cash. The swaps would then be cancelled.

Simultaneously, the two parties would transact a small number of swaps that have an overall risk profile very similar to that of the cancelled portfolio. Because of this similarity, there would be almost no change in either party's risk profile. But the new swaps would be *on market*, i.e. their fixed legs would be at current market prices, so there would be no outstanding credit risk. Note that this recouponing is voluntary, in that neither party is legally obliged to agree to cancel the old swaps, or to transact the new ones. However, it is a matter of convention and courtesy between swap traders that such recouponing is done, and is done near mid-market prices.

The fourth credit-improvement strategy is SwapClear, a service provided by the London Clearing House (LCH). This is a clearing service similar to that used on futures exchanges. If JPM is to receive fixed from CSFB, and both parties agree to use Swap-Clear, then JPM will receive from the London Clearing House, which will receive from CSFB. SwapClear is margined, in that the LCH takes enough margin from each of its counterparties to cover the total of current exposure and the additional exposure that might result from a one-day move. However, SwapClear is not available for all swap market participants, nor for all types of swap.

Cross-currency basis swaps

We have seen that an interest-rate swap is just an exchange of deposits. Most of the cashflows in these two deposits cancel, and hence the credit risk on this exchange is very much smaller than on a bond. In the previous example, the two deposits were in the same currency; this ensured that the initial and final exchanges of principals cancelled.

But as well as switching bonds from fixed rate to floating rate, or vice versa, it is also useful to switch between currencies. The key tool for this is the *cross-currency basis swap*, usually abbreviated to *basis swap*. A basis swap is effectively an exchange of floating-rate deposits in different currencies.

Again let us assume that JPM and CSFB have traded. Let us assume that JPM is depositing sterling with CSFB, which is depositing dollars with JPM, and that these deposits are for 10 years, with quarterly interest payments. The *price* of the basis swap is conventionally quoted as an adjustment to interest payments on the non-USD leg: let us assume that the price is –5bp. So CSFB deposits dollars with JPM at USD Libor, and JPM is depositing sterling with CSFB at Libor – 5bp. There will be a sequence of payments in two currencies:

- In sterling there will be an initial deposit, periodic interest payments, and at maturity a return of the principal. So at the start, JPM deposits £100 million with CSFB. Every three months thereafter, CSFB makes interest payments to JPM, calculated using a rate of 3-month GBP Libor – 5bp. At maturity, CSFB repays the £100 million.
- In dollars there will also be an initial deposit, periodic interest payments, and at maturity a return of the principal. The dollar amount is the same value as the sterling amount; if the GBP/USD rate were 1.50, the dollar amount would be $150 million. CSFB deposits this amount with JPM, which then makes interest payments to CSFB calculated at 3-month USD Libor exactly. At maturity, JPM returns the dollar principal.

Let us briefly summarise this basis swap. A typical basis swap is an exchange of deposits in which both sides are floating. In this case CSFB deposits dollars with JPM. CSFB receives interest payments on this deposit, calculated at USD Libor exactly, and at maturity CSFB is returned the USD principal. JPM deposits sterling with CSFB. The interest payments on this non-dollar deposit are calculated using the appropriate IBOR ± a spread. This spread is the price of the basis swap. At maturity JPM is returned the principal.

The price of a basis swap

So a cross-currency basis swap is an exchange of deposits: one in dollars at Libor exactly and one in a non-dollar currency at IBOR ± a spread. What determines this spread, this price of a basis swap?

In theory the spread reflects the difference in the creditworthiness of the banks in the fixing panels. The easiest way to visualise this is to consider two fixing panels in the same currency. Let us imagine that the panel of banks in the fixing of JPY Libor consists of only top-notch banks, but that the Tibor panel consists of only weak banks. (This characterisation of the London and Tokyo yen panels is only partly true, but is helpful for this explanation.)

Further, let us assume that the weak banks can borrow money only by paying 10bp more than a top-notch bank, and it is known that this will always be the case. In this scenario, Tibor will always be 10bp above JPY Libor, so the fair value of the basis swap would be to exchange JPY Libor for Tibor – 10bp. Indeed, at this price, all the payments in the swap would be zero.

So, if the market price for a GBP basis swap of some maturity is –5bp, then the market is saying that the GBP fixing panel consists, or will consist, of banks that are slightly weaker than the banks in the USD panel.

More often than not, in practice this theory is completely useless. Actually, the price of a basis swap is driven purely by supply and demand. As we shall see, basis swaps are used when investors want assets in one currency but borrowers want to issue in another. For example, many investors want sterling-denominated assets, and this demand—rather than any belief about the creditworthiness of the banks in the GBP panel—explains the negative price of the sterling basis swap.

A cross-currency issue

The next few diagrams show the cashflows associated with a corporate bond issue. We assume that the bond is fixed-coupon sterling but that the issuer actually wants to borrow floating-rate US dollars. For simplicity, we assume the price of the bond is par; if this weren't so, the payments would be even more complicated.

At the start, the investor pays for the bond in sterling. The borrower wants to borrow dollars not sterling, so deposits the sterling with the investment bank, which in turn gives a return deposit of the same value of US dollars (the diagram assumes an FX rate of 1.50). So, as wanted, the borrower is borrowing dollars.

**A fixed-rate sterling bond swapped to dollar floating:
cashflows at issue**

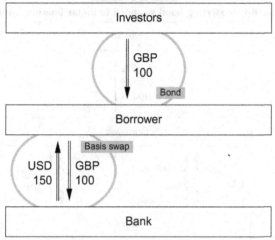

Next we show the interest payments. The borrower has contracted to pay fixed-coupon sterling to the investors; assume this coupon is 5.50%. An interest-rate swap converts this to GBP Libor; the borrower receives fixed from the investment bank, and pays floating. Finally, the basis swap converts these payments of floating GBP to floating USD.

Note the slightly unusual feature of the basis swap. When two swap dealers trade a basis swap, there is no spread on the USD Libor leg, but there is a spread on the non-USD leg. In the diagram it is the other way round, with the GBP Libor leg at flat and the USD leg holding the spread. Why? Because that is what the client wants. Whatever the standard payment streams, they are often altered to meet a client's requirements. This client, the borrower, wants to borrow USD, paying coupons of USD Libor ± spread. So the level of the GBP interest-rate swap is set to equal the coupon on the bond, and the price of the whole package is absorbed in the spread on the USD leg.

A fixed-rate sterling bond swapped to dollar floating: coupons

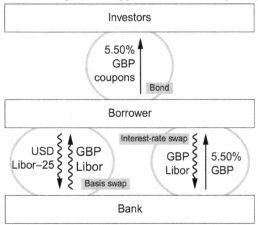

Finally comes the repayment of the principal of the bond. This is just the reverse of the initial payments.

A fixed-rate sterling bond swapped to dollar floating: the principal

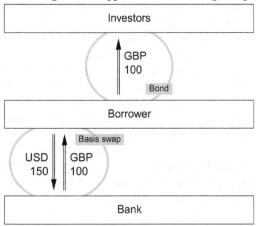

So, in summary, the investors have bought a fixed-coupon sterling bond; the borrower is borrowing floating-rate US dollars; and the investment bank is left holding the difference between these payment streams.

Reducing credit risk in basis swaps

Cross-currency swaps are a highly credit-intensive derivative structure. Consider the situation in which a company, the borrower in the previous example, has deposited £100 million with an investment bank, and the investment bank has deposited $150 million with the company. At the time this was done, the GBP/USD exchange rate, known as *cable*, was at 1.50, so these two deposits were of similar value. Now imagine that sterling falls to $1.40. The investment bank's deposit with the company is now worth $10 million more than the company's deposit at the bank. If the company were to fold, the bank would be $10 million out of pocket; this is the size of the credit exposure.

When banks trade basis swaps with each other, they use the credit mitigation techniques described in the context of interest-rate swaps, plus one additional technique. At the start of each coupon period, the dollar side of the basis swap is resized to match the current FX rate. So if cable were still equal to 1.40 (GBP/USD=1.40) at the start of the next coupon period, $10 million of the outstanding $150 million deposit would be returned, and the two legs of the transaction would then be of the same value (£100 million and $140 million).

However, many non-financial companies do not want to be in the position of suddenly being required to find $10 million, so they insist on a *constant notional* dollar leg. The bank's best strategy is to be careful in its choice of customers, to judge their creditworthiness ruthlessly, and to ensure that the profitability of the trades justifies the size of the credit lines.

Forward rate agreements

We have already discussed interest-rate swaps and cross-currency basis swaps. Among the other types of swap is the forward rate agreement (FRA). A FRA is similar to a one-period interest-rate swap.

Consider such a one-period swap, denominated in Swiss francs, starting 18 September 2008, ending 18 March 2009, with a fixed leg of 3.50% and a floating leg of 6-month CHF Libor. This swap has only one interest period, and two days before its start, on Tuesday 16 September 2008, 6-month CHF Libor is observed. The interest on a deposit at this floating rate is calculated, as is the interest on a deposit at the fixed rate of 3.50%. In an interest-rate swap, the losing party would pay the difference between these two sums on 18 March 2009.

But if the trade had been a FRA, rather than waiting 6 months before paying, the present value of this sum would be paid at the start of the deposit period, on 18 September 2008. The amount paid would be the difference between the two interest payments, discounted back to the start; and this discounting is at the floating interest rate.

So a FRA is much like a one-period swap, except that the loser pays at the start rather than at the end. If today is 18 Aug 2008, the FRA would be called a 'CHF 1×7', as it is in Swiss francs, starting in 1 month and ending in 7 months. If today were a different day in August 2008, the FRA would be described as 'CHF 1×7 out of the 18th'.

Summary

- Swaps are not devoid of credit risk.
- There are various credit mitigation strategies available, but some types of swap user are not willing to accept them.
- A basis swap is effectively an exchange of floating-rate deposits in different currencies.

SWAPS REVISITED

- Basis swaps allow assets or liabilities to be converted between currencies.
- Cross-currency basis swaps can be constant notional or variable notional.
- An FRA is a one-period swap that pays at the start rather than at the end.

Chapter 11

Non-government issuance

Introduction

Governments issue most of their debt at auction. Most governments specify a calendar of auctions, typically covering the fiscal year. A few weeks or days before an auction, the size and maturity are announced. If it is a new bond, trading of it begins then. This is known as *when-issued* (WI) or *grey market* trading. When-issued trades settle (money being exchanged for bond) on the same day that the auction itself settles.

Those eligible to bid—in most markets the primary dealers—submit bids by the appropriate time. There is a delay while these bids are sorted into order of decreasing price, after which the issuing government announces the cutoff price. Bids above this are accepted, bids below are declined, and those at the cutoff are accepted in part.

The auction mechanism works well enough for frequent borrowers, whose names are widely known in the markets, and whose credit is widely understood. But the situation is quite different for a smaller or less frequent borrower. Imagine that a medium-sized American industrial company is going to borrow $200 million for 5 years. One might expect pension funds or insurers to hold this bond in *clips* of $2 million to $10 million. These are small amounts, too small to justify the substantial research that would be required to assess the company's credit.

Instead an investment bank assists in the issuance of the corporate bond, *bringing the deal to market* on behalf of its client, the issuer.

Bringing a deal to market

The process is started by the client, who must choose a bank. The choice might be made competitively, with different banks engaging in a *beauty contest* or tendering the price at which they believe the company could borrow. Alternatively, the choice might be made on the basis of a pre-existing banking relationship, perhaps related to some other transaction, such as a takeover. Use of a pre-existing relationship has the advantage of avoiding any further sharing of confidential information.

In this phase the client will deal with the debt origination department or a department with a similar name. The debt origination department is behind the Chinese wall; its work is confidential, and public side traders, salespeople and researchers will not know of these consultations. The origination group gives advice to the client on how much debt it should have, and in what form. This advice makes allowance for law, tax and the company's long-term objectives.

Once it has been decided to borrow money via a bond issue, it will be announced that the bank has been *mandated* by the would-be issuer. Some mandate announcements specify the size and term of the borrowing, such as EUR 250 million for 5 years, but they are not always specified, as in this example.

NON-GOVERNMENT ISSUANCE

```
08:12 14MAR01           SCREEN INSIDER              UK41974

- AVENTIS has mandated CSFB, DRESDNER KW and SG INVESTMENT
BANKING to lead manage an inaugural EURO benchmark issue. The
issue will be launched, subject to market conditions, following
a European roadshow planned for the end of this month. AVENTIS
is a world leader in pharmaceuticals and agriculture.
```

At the time of the announcement the *syndicate desk* will become involved. The syndicate desk arranges the issue for the borrower. However, unlike the debt origination department, the syndicate desk is on the public side of the Chinese wall; it has no inside information.

Once the mandate has been announced, the syndicate desk involves several other teams. Credit research assesses the borrower, and if they aren't already rated, it may assign some form of rating. Typically, a research note is constructed, detailing the company and its financial strengths and weaknesses, and comparing it to competitors and other similarly rated borrowers.

Salespeople speak to their clients and try to discover at what price the end-investors will buy the bond. For a fixed-rate bond, this will usually be quoted as a spread over government bonds: if a yield of govt + 200bp is too little, perhaps the clients will accept govt + 210bp.

Interest-rate traders become involved, especially if the issuance is to be swapped into another form. For example, if the issue is to be fixed-rate EUR but the borrower wants to borrow floating-rate USD, then there will be a need for a euro interest-rate swap to convert fixed EUR to floating EUR, and for a basis swap to convert floating EUR to floating USD.

For a new borrower, whose name is not known to investors in that currency, there may also be a *roadshow*. This will typically take the form of a series of meetings between investors, and on the other side, an official from the borrower, and a salesperson and a credit analyst from the bank bringing the deal to market.

The syndicate desk coordinates the work of these teams with each other and with the borrowers. Its job can be political, especially if the borrower is unwilling to pay a spread large enough to persuade investors to lend.

The syndicate

Several banks can be involved in bringing a deal to market, collectively known as the *syndicate*, after which the syndicate desk is named. The chief bank in the syndicate is known as the *book-runner* or *lead manager*, or sometimes the *global coordinator*; usage is not consistent.

Besides selling bonds, the syndicate agrees to use reasonable endeavours to make a market in the issue after it has been placed. This agreement is not intended to be legally enforceable, but is an understanding, insisted upon by the investors. If a lead manager were to sell a bond to a client and subsequently be unwilling to make a price in that bond, the client would quickly become an ex-client.

Some banks take a junior position within the syndicate. These banks, known as *co-leads*, *co-managers* or *managers*, are allocated bonds to sell but they have no subsequent market-making obligations. They take the smallest slice of any fees. Sometimes there are co-leads and co-managers (or senior and junior co-leads); there is little difference between the two, except that the co-leads will have a larger allocation of bonds, and their names will appear more prominently on the prospectus.

The book-runner's choice of the rest of the selling group, and of the allocation of bonds, is necessarily political. The chosen banks are usually competitors, but for the purposes of this deal cooperation is necessary. There is a fair amount of mutual backscratching; if I never invite you into my deals, you will never invite me into yours. Further, the lead managers will want as complete a coverage as possible: for example, there would be no point in having five banks with excellent sales coverage in Germany but none in the UK.

Book-building: taking orders

The selling group has now been chosen, and each bank now speaks to its clients about the deal. There isn't yet a fixed price for the debt, but there may be a fixed spread over the government yield, or failing that, at least an indicative spread. So it is known that the debt will be issued at govt + 205bp, say, but the price of the reference government bond is not known.

Clients wanting bonds will undertake to buy at the issue spread, or will leave an indication in spread terms such as 'if the spread is not less than +205bp, I'll take €15 million'. This order-taking process is called *book-building*: the banks try to sell their quota of bonds in advance. If a bank fails to sell its quota, it may have to take the bonds onto its own book—a necessary risk but certainly not a desired outcome.

It may be that the book-building process is a quick sell-out. In this case there will be a discussion with the borrower, and the deal may well be expanded. If so, the lead manager will announce the new larger deal size on the wire services. In this example, let us imagine that the original €250 million deal was fully sold and then enlarged to €350 million, with the whole size being sold at govt + 205bp.

However, it may be that the deal is oversubscribed but is not to be expanded, or not to be expanded further. In this case purchases will be scaled back. The lead managers decide by how much each of the selling bank's allotment is to be below demand; each member of the selling group decides by how much to scale back each client's allotment. The selling bank then makes an offer of allotment to the investor, who either accepts it or refuses it.

An increasingly common variation is the *pot syndicate*. Here all the orders are put into a single metaphorical pot, and the allocation of bonds is done from the centre by the lead managers. This increases the control and hence the accountability of the lead managers, but it reduces the accountability of the co-managers.

Whichever syndicate structure is used, the issue is sold at a price quoted as a spread over a reference government bond. It will next be necessary to determine the price of this government bond, and if the new issue is to be swapped, to determine the price of the swap. Their synchronisation has interesting and important market consequences.

Pricing a swapped deal

For simplicity, assume that the book-runner is the only bank in the selling group, and assume that the €350 million fixed-coupon deal is being swapped into floating-rate USD, a common arrangement. What are the book-runner's flows? The book-runner is to receive the new corporate bond from the issuer, and to pass it on to the investors. So, assuming it to be fully sold, this does not contribute to any net flow for the book-runner.

With the issuer, the book-runner will be paying (i.e. paying fixed and receiving floating) in size €350 million. The investment bank is also trading a basis swap, but the price of a basis swap moves slowly, so this risk is much less and is ignored here.

The investor side is more mixed. Some investors will be paying for the new bond out of cash. Others will find the cash to buy the new bond by selling a different bond. Recall that the new bond will be quoted as a spread: a specific government bond plus so many basis points (205 in this case). Many investors generate the cash to buy the new bond by selling this particular government bond, a strategy which has the added benefit of almost entirely eliminating their interest-rate risk in the transaction. So the book-runner will be getting back the various old bonds which are being sold by the investors. As an example, let us assume that the investors are providing €150 million of new money and selling €200 million of old bonds.

So all in, the investment bank is buying €200 million of bonds from investors, and paying fixed on €350 million of swap. The total effect is that the bank is selling fixed-income assets (equivalent to selling bonds or paying swaps). And the price at which the investment bank would most like to do this selling is a high price.

So the investment bank needs to buy and it wants the market price to be high; and conveniently the buying can easily cause a high price. So the investment bank buys back the €150 million of bonds it requires. The buying is timed so that the moment of *pricing* is just as the market price reaches its buying-induced maximum.

So just before the deal is priced, the investment bank will be buying bonds. At the moment that the deal is priced, the high price of the government bond is observed in the market, and published. This is converted to a yield, the issue spread is added, and this yield converted into a price of the new bond. This is the *reoffer price*, and the deal is said to be *priced*. Those investors that have agreed to buy bonds do so either against the government bond or out of cash.

There are, however, two constraints on the pricing. First, if the price of the government bond is driven up excessively high, then more investors will buy the new bond out of an old bond rather than out of new money. Second, the investment bank's competitors can use any price distortion as a selling opportunity. Nonetheless, just before and at the moment of pricing a swapped new issue, the government bond market can trade expensively, particularly in the maturity of the new deal.

Pricing an unswapped deal

Similar reasoning leads to the opposite outcome for an unswapped deal. The investment bank will be buying the new bond from the issuer and selling it to the investors. For the investment bank there is no net flow here. But some investors will be selling old bonds to buy the new one. Purchasing the old bonds would leave the investment bank long and needing to sell. Again the optimum time for this transaction is just before pricing. So the investment bank sells just before pricing, and thus buys bonds from the investors at a cheap price. Similar constraints apply: if the market is too soft, investors will put new cash to work rather than selling old bonds, and the investment bank's competitors will be happy to use any artificial weakness as an opportunity to buy cheap bonds.

Some legal details

Corporate debt is awash with legal detail. Some of this is driven by US law, especially the Securities Act 1933, and some by commercial considerations.

Every bond has a governing law. The most common jurisdiction is that of England and Wales, followed by New York and then Germany. If the issuer defaults, judgement is given in accordance with the law of the governing jurisdiction.

A bond may be a domestic bond, a eurobond or a global. A *domestic bond* is entirely within one jurisdiction. The issuer, the investment bank, the stock exchange on which it is listed and the investors to which it is being sold lie within the same country. Domestics are most often German, American or Swiss.

A *eurobond* is a multi-country instrument, offered outside the country of the issuer, sometimes known as a eurosecurity. It will not be registered with the US regulator, the Securities and Exchange Commission (SEC). Because it is not registered with the SEC, it may not be sold to most US investors, at least initially. There are various exceptions, including SEC rule 144A, which allows the bond to be sold to certain large US investors, known as Qualified Institutional Buyers (QIBs), subject to documentation and other rules. Non-QIB US investors who wish to buy have to wait until after the *seasoning date*, which is usually when the bond has been in existence 40 days. Note that here the word 'euro' does not refer to the currency of the eurozone.

A *global* will have been registered with the SEC, so it may be sold in the US as well as in (most of) the rest of the world. Registering is slow and expensive, so it tends to be worthwhile only for frequent borrowers, such as the World Bank, and for US-based issuers. Confusingly, some eurobonds to which rule 144A applies are colloquially known as globals, because they can be sold to QIB investors in the US.

Most bonds have *selling restrictions* prohibiting the sale of the bond to private investors in certain countries. Selling restrictions are usually motivated by tax and securities laws. Usual restrictions are the US, the country of the issuer, the country of the underwriter, and the country of the governing law. Selling restrictions do not apply to institutional investors.

A bearer bond or note is a physical piece of paper, much like a banknote, and is owned by whoever holds it. Some private investors, particularly in Austria and Belgium, like to hold bonds in bearer form. Most issuers do not go to the expense of printing a large number of bearer bonds, but some do and these retail-sized bearer bonds are described as *definitive bearer notes*. In dollars, euros and sterling the typical denominations are 1k, 10k and 100k. Written on the notes with the terms and conditions will be the name and address of a *paying agent*, a bank that is paid by the issuer and then handles the administration of the payments of coupons and principal.

Every bond, whether bearer or registered, will have a prospectus or equivalent, detailing the terms. The prospectus might apply only to that particular bond, or might be written in more general terms to cover a range of debt instruments. Whichever, when a new bond is announced some of the terms will be summarised concisely using standard acronyms, of which three are worth mentioning here.

NP is *Negative Pledge*. The handbook of the International Primary Markets Association (IPMA) says that:

> A negative pledge is normally given by the issuer ... to ensure that other creditors do not obtain a better claim to assets on liquidation. The essence of the undertaking is not to create ... any mortgage ... over any present or future assets.

So if the issuer subsequently goes into liquidation, no other creditor has a prior claim on the issuer's assets. Subordinated issues will not have a negative pledge.

XD is *Cross Default*, which says that defaulting to one is defaulting to all. Consider the position of an investor who owns a bond that pays coupons every 15 June. Some weeks after a coupon, in July, the issuer suddenly goes bankrupt. It will be 11 months before there is a default to the holder of the June-paying bond. Creditors have various legal rights upon default, and the investor will not want to wait 11 months before being able to exercise those rights. A cross-default clause accelerates the exercisability of those rights. A cross-default clause may extend to defaults of a guarantor, and may have exclusions, such as for defaults involving only tiny sums of money.

FM is *Force Majeure*. Typically a new deal settles (money is exchanged for bond) two weeks after it is priced. If, at any time before the new issue settles,

> in the opinion of the Lead Manager, there shall have been such a change in national or international financial, political or economic conditions or currency exchange rates or exchange controls as would in their view be likely to prejudice materially the success of the offering

then the lead manager can cite Force Majeure and cancel the issue. This happens extremely rarely.

Free to trade

During the book-building process, the lead managers only sell the new debt at the agreed yield spread over the reference bond. Once the book-building is complete, investors are informed of how many bonds they have been allotted—the amount they requested minus any scale-back. After allocation the bond becomes *free to trade*, with its price being determined by the usual market forces of buyers and sellers.

Although the official agreement is that lead managers only sell debt at the official spread, there can be a little room for manoeuvre. If a client wants to buy the new bond by selling an old bond, it can happen that a lead manager will be willing to buy the old bond at a slightly generous price, thus effectively subsidising the purchase of the new bond.

Once free to trade, the ideal result is for the bond to tighten in a few basis points relative to the government bond. So if it were issued at +205bp, and on becoming free to trade were to improve to +203bp, that would be deemed a highly successful issue. If instead it were to widen, say to +215bp, then the investors would lose money, leaving them unhappy. The opposite case is not much better. If the new bond were to tighten very far, say to +150bp, then the issuer could have borrowed money much more cheaply, and will not be impressed by the lead managers' advice. From the viewpoint of the lead managers, the worst result would be that most of the bonds are unsold, remain with the lead managers, and then cheapen with the spread widening hugely.

An example issue

```
14:40 08MAR01          SCREEN INSIDER              UK41974

The STG 175m straight issue for COCA COLA ENTERPRISES INC,
rated A2/A (stable), is now priced. Due 7 December 2016, the
deal pays a coupon of 6.5% and has an issue/reoffer price of
98.897, to give a spread of 175bp over 8% 2015 Gilt. Lead
manager is CSFB. Co-leads are HSBC and UBS WARBURG. Fees total
50bp, split 30bp selling, 20bp m + u. Pay 15 March. Listing Lux.
Denoms 1k + 10k + 100k. US/UK limits. Tefra-D2. NP, XD and FM. NY
law. Std tax. Launched under the issuer's MTN programme. The
deal will be offered via PrimeDebt, CSFB's internet offering
system.
```

This announcement should now start to make sense. The bond is issued by Coca Cola Enterprises Inc, rated A2 by Moody's and A by Standard & Poor's. Neither rating agency has this issuer on watch for an upgrade or downgrade; the rating is stable. Of size £175 million, the bond pays a coupon of 6.5% and matures on 07 December 2016. The issue price is 98.897, so it yields +175bp more than the 8% December 2015 gilt (which was trading in the market at 134.00 just before this announcement).

The lead manager is CSFB, with HSBC and UBS Warburg as co-leads. Fees are 0.50% of the cash raised, split 0.30% for selling and 0.20% for management and underwriting. The fees can be somewhat fictitious, as they would be included in the funding cost that CSFB would have quoted to the issuer.

The settlement date, on which bond is exchanged for cash, is 15 March. Listed on the Luxembourg Stock Exchange, it is available in bearer form, in multiples of £1000. UK selling limits apply, as do US limits (known as TEFRA). The bond has negative pledge, cross-default and force majeure clauses, and is issued under the law of New York, with a standard tax clause. The issuer has a medium-term note programme, which includes a generic prospectus that can be used for many individual bond issues, and that prospectus applies here.

Opportunistic reopenings

The previous section describes the full process by which new bonds are brought to market. But this can be greatly shortened for well-known issuers. Many supranational issuers have a funding target, and they borrow whenever they can borrow cheaper than this target. Most supranationals have a funding target in floating-rate dollars, such as USD Libor − 35bp, though a small number of funding targets are euro-denominated.

Let us assume that an investment bank believes it can sell a further tranche of an already existing bond at a sufficiently low yield that the all-in cost of borrowing is no more expensive than the funding target. The investment bank would then contact the relevant supranational and an issue would most probably follow soon after. There would not be a roadshow or a mandate announcement; instead there would be a single announcement after pricing.

Summary

- Several banks cooperate in bringing a new deal to market.
- Book-building entails selling bonds in advance.
- Pricing a fixed-coupon new issue can distort the market. If the issue is swapped, the market may become artificially expensive; if the issue is unswapped, the market may become artificially cheap.
- Issues of debt come with much legal detail, driven by tax laws and US regulation.
- Some frequent issuers do so opportunistically, using a much shortened procedure.

Chapter 12

Yield, duration, repo and forward bond prices

Measuring risk

Bonds can change in price. Owning a bond is not riskless—prices can and do move. It seems natural to ask how risky a bond is. Indeed, how risky is any portfolio of bonds? A full treatment of this question is far beyond the scope of this book, but it is reasonably easy to make a start.

As an example, let us consider a particular bond: 10-year maturity and an annual coupon of 6%. There will be a market price for this bond. If it costs 100 then its yield will be 6%. Equivalently, if its yield is 6% then it must cost 100.

A little calculation shows that if the bond yield falls 0.01% to 5.99%, then the price rises by 7.3636¢. And if the bond yield were to rise by the same amount, the price would fall by 7.3566¢. So a 0.01% change in the yield moves the price by about 0.0736% in the opposite direction. More concisely, the price moves about 7.36 times faster than the yield.

This ratio is known as the *duration* of a bond. For a 2-year bond with an annual coupon of 6% the duration is about 1.8, for a 5-year bond about 4.2, for a 10-year bond about 7.4 (as we have seen) and for a 30-year bond about 13.8. So the price of a 30-year 6% bond moves almost 14 times as fast as its yield: a positive 10bp change in the yield will drop the price by about 1.4%.

Duration is a very useful concept, but awkwardly comes in several different flavours. But before we consider these, we need to look more closely at yield.

Yields: compounding frequencies

Many prices can be quoted in different ways. For instance, one might buy oil by volume or by weight. Because oil comes in different grades and types, there is no single conversion factor between the two, but in any given case one quotation method can be converted into another. Likewise, a yield can be quoted in one of several ways. The difference between them is 'optical' rather than fundamental, in that 8% quoted one way may be the same as 8.16% quoted another way.

Consider a bank deposit that pays 8% at the end of the year: $100 at the start would become $108 at the end. Another bank might quote the same rate of interest but make payments semi-annually. Clearly this would be preferable from the depositor's viewpoint, because the depositor is paid interest on the interest: $100 at the start of the year becomes $108.16 at the end (this being a $100 principal, $8 of interest on this, and $0.16 of interest on the first interest payment). So 8% quoted *semi-annual*, or *semi*, is the same as 8.16% quoted *annual*.

Interest rates can be quoted quarterly. A $100 deposit that pays 8% quarterly will be worth $100 \times 1.02 = \$102$ after one quarter, $100 \times 1.02^2 = \$104.04$ after half a year, $100 \times 1.02^3 = \$106.1208$ after nine months and a grand $100 \times 1.02^4 =$

$108.243216 at the end of 1 year. So 8% quarterly is equivalent to just over 8.243% annual.

There is an extreme case of this, much used by financial mathematicians. Consider paying interest, not annually, not monthly, not daily or even hourly, but continuously. A little mathematics can show that 8% *continuously compounded* is the same as 8.3287% annual.[†] It happens that the continuously compounded yield is the easiest form of yield to manipulate mathematically. Fortunately for the non-mathematicians, after the equations are done the answer is usually translated back into a more intuitive form.

We saw earlier that 8% quoted semi-annual is 8.16% annual. The table provides a ready reckoner for such conversions. Choose the column containing the desired conversion and the row containing the starting yield, then the table entry is the number of basis points (units of 0.01%) to add. For example, to convert 6% semi-annual to annual, add 9bp.

	Semi to Ann	Qrtly to Semi	Qrtly to Ann
0%	0.0	0.0	0.0
1%	0.2	0.1	0.4
2%	1.0	0.5	1.5
3%	2.2	1.1	3.4
4%	4.0	2.0	6.0
5%	6.2	3.1	9.5
6%	9.0	4.5	13.6
7%	12.2	6.1	18.6
8%	16.0	8.0	24.3
9%	20.2	10.1	30.8
10%	25.0	12.5	38.1
12%	36.0	18.0	55.1

[†] Mathematically, the relationship between these different yields can be summarised as $(1 + r_{annual}) = (1 + r_{semi-annual}/2)^2 = (1 + r_{quarterly}/4)^4 = \exp(r_{continuous})$.

The explanation of compounding frequencies started by looking at a deposit. Actually, in the wholesale market, deposit rates are quoted *simple*, which means that the compounding frequency is the same as the term of the deposit. So a 1-year deposit is quoted annual, a 6-month deposit semi-annual, a 4-month deposit tri-annual, and a 3-month deposit quarterly.

This is not true for long-dated bonds, which have a yield convention that does not vary with maturity. US Treasuries, British gilts and Australian Commonwealth governments bonds pay semi-annual coupons, and have yields quoted semi-annual. So a 6% bond costing par will have a yield of 6% semi-annual.

Switzerland, Sweden, Denmark and most eurozone governments have bonds that pay one coupon per annum and have yields quoted annual. So a conversion is needed to compare US or British government yields to those of Germany or Switzerland. If all the yields are quoted conventionally, they are not comparable. Either the US and British yields should be converted to annual, or the European yields to semi-annual.

Italy and Japan are more awkward cases. Italian fixed-coupon government bonds (BTPs) pay a semi-annual coupon, but their yields are conventionally quoted annual. So a 6% BTP costing 100 will have a quoted annual yield of 6.09%. Japanese government bonds have their own convention, not used anywhere else. It is not compatible with or easily converted to any other more sensible convention, and hence is often ignored and replaced by the US semi-annual convention.

Duration continued

Recall that we were developing a numerical measure of risk for a bond, and that this numerical measure showed the percentage price change per change in yield. But change in which yield? If a bond yields 8% semi-annual, this is 8.16% annual. A 0.01% increase in the semi-annual yield is a 0.01040025% increase in the annual yield. So, at this level of yields, the annual yield moves 1.04 times faster than the semi-annual yield.

And hence there must be different measures of duration, according to the convention in which yields are quoted. And of these measures, the most elegant is called Macaulay duration, after its inventor. Unfortunately, it assumes that yields are quoted in the least intuitive form—continuously compounded.

Consider a bond that pays a single cashflow in n years' time. Its Macaulay duration is simply n. A small decrease in the continuously compounded yield will increase the price by n times as much. The decrease in yield is quoted in percent per annum; multiplying this by the number of years gives the price change as a percentage of the price.

Now consider a 10-year bond paying annual coupons of 6%. For analytic purposes we can consider this bond as the sum of its cashflows: $100 of the bond is really $6 of a 1-year cashflow plus $6 of a 2-year cashflow plus … plus $106 of a 10-year cashflow. So the duration of this bond will be the average, weighted somehow, of the times of payments of the cashflows.

A little mathematics shows that Macaulay duration of a bond is just the weighted average of the times of payments of the cashflows, where the weights are the present values of the cashflows.[†] For this reason Macaulay duration is often known as *average life*: some payments come soon, some late; on average they arrive after the amount of time known as Macaulay duration.

So Macaulay duration is the sensitivity per unit cash to a move in the continuously compounded yield. Modified duration is easily computed from Macaulay duration; it is the sensitivity per unit cash to a move in the conventionally quoted yield.[‡]

[†] Assume that a bond makes payments c_i at times t_i, and has a continuously compounded yield r if purchased for delivery at time 0. The dirty price of this bond including accrued interest, which we call p, therefore satisfies $p = \sum c_i \exp(-rt_i)$. Observe that $\partial p/\partial r = -\sum t_i c_i \exp(-rt_i)$. Let the present value of cashflow i be $w_i = c_i \exp(-rt_i)$, so the risk per unit money is $-(1/p)\partial p/\partial r = (\sum t_i w_i)/(\sum w_i)$; this is the weighted average of the times of payments of the cashflows, where the weights are the present values of the cashflows. Thus the Macaulay duration is indeed the average life.

[‡] Modified duration = Macaulay duration $\div (1 + y/n)$ where y is the conventionally quoted yield and n is the compounding frequency for that yield; $n = 1$ for annual, $n = 2$ for semi-annual.

Duration is important. Interest-rate traders, of all types, always control their duration carefully, and will always know how many dollars of profit or loss would be caused by a 0.01% drop in yields.

Definition of DV01

We have now met Macaulay duration. This is both the average life of a bond and the sensitivity per unit cash to a move in the continuously compounded yield. We have also met modified duration, which is the sensitivity per unit cash to a move in the conventionally quoted yield. Both of these are sensitivities per unit cash. A related concept is DV01, which is the Dollar Value of an 'oh one', or a 0.01% move in the yield.

DV01 is the sensitivity of the price of a bond to a 1bp move in the conventionally quoted yield. Note that DV01, unlike duration, is per 100 nominal not per 100 cash value. And hence a bond with a dirty price of say 140 will have a DV01 that is 1.4 times as large as its modified duration. Sometimes DV01 is quoted for the actual size of the holding rather than for 100 nominal. The context usually makes obvious which is happening.

How coupon affects duration and DV01

To further illustrate the difference between duration and DV01, it is helpful to ask about the effect of coupon. Consider two bonds with the same maturity and yield, one of which has a higher coupon. Would this bond have a higher DV01? A higher duration?

Let us consider the DV01 first. Consider 100 nominal of the higher-coupon bond as being 100 nominal of the lower-coupon bond plus some additional cashflows, these being the extra coupon amounts. Clearly, the additional cashflows will have price risk, in that a higher yield will diminish their present value. So the higher-coupon bond will have a larger DV01.

But duration is measured per 100 value. The higher-coupon bond will have a larger price than the lower-coupon bond, as it consists of larger cashflows. So someone who invests 100 of money in the higher-coupon bond will in effect be buying more of the coupons but less of the principal. But the coupons are shorter in maturity than the principal, or at least no longer. So the average maturity of cashflow bought by this 100 units of money will be shorter in the higher-coupon bond, and hence the higher-coupon bond will have the lower duration.

In summary a higher coupon implies a higher DV01 but a lower duration.

An example yield curve

Now we have the concepts of duration and DV01 it becomes possible to discuss a yield-curve trade. The following chart shows part of the US Treasury yield curve as of the close on 14 October 1999.

The three bonds discussed in the examples below have been highlighted. These are the 3-year, with a 6.25% coupon and maturing on 31 August 2002; the 5-year 6% 15 Aug 2004; and the 10-year 6% 15 Aug 2009. As of the close of business (cob) on 14 October 1999 these three had prices of 100-23 (i.e. $100\frac{23}{32}$), 99-24+ (i.e. $99\frac{24}{32} + \frac{1}{64}$) and 98-28, and hence they had yields of 5.971%, 6.054% and 6.153%.

First, observe that the curve is broadly positive: longer-dated bonds yield more than shorter-dated bonds. In particular, 3s5s is +8.3bp, and 5s10s is +9.9bp.

Second, observe that the 5- and 10-year are expensive (low-yielding) relative to similar-maturity USTs. One might think that this should be arbitraged away, with holders of these bonds selling them, and instead acquiring the cheaper (higher-yielding) bonds of similar maturity. But this would miss part of the story. These two bonds are special in repo; they have repo rates that are lower than the general collateral rates of most other USTs. So holders of these two bonds receive what can be thought of as a rebate to compensate for their expensiveness, and this rebate comes in the form of being able to borrow money cheaply. Further, these bonds will also be more liquid, that is, they can be bought and sold in larger size at lower transaction cost, and hence are known as *benchmarks*, or *on-the-runs*. Part of the expensiveness of the 5- and 10-year benchmarks may reflect the market value of that ease of transaction.

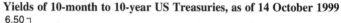

Yields of 10-month to 10-year US Treasuries, as of 14 October 1999

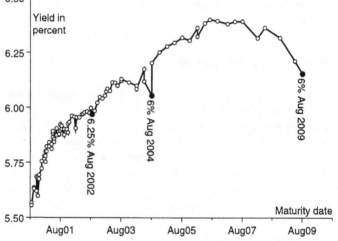

A 3s10s flattener

Let us move on. The 10-year bond yields +18.2bp more than the 3-year. If a trader thought that the yield curve was set to flatten, i.e. that this 18.2bp gap was likely to reduce or even become negative, what would be the correct trade?

Clearly, the trader must buy some of the 10-year and sell some of the 3-year. But how much 3-year for each $100 of

10-year? If the 10-year outperforms the 3-year, then the trade should make money. But if the curve moves in parallel (i.e if both the bonds in the trade gain or lose the same amount of yield), the trade should break even. This requirement allows the ratio to be calculated.

A typical trading floor will have many calculators able to assist with the arithmetic, but in this example the calculations were done using the YA function on a widely used system called Bloomberg. For the 10-year, a 1bp change in yield changes the price by 7.25¢; for the 3-year 2.62¢. So, if the trader were to buy $100 nominal of the 10-year and sell $100 × (7.25/2.62) ≈ $276.72 nominal of the 3-year, then a parallel move in the curve (both bonds up or down in yield by the same amount) would neither make nor lose money. This is therefore the correct ratio.

This calculation was done using the DV01s and the nominal amounts of each bond. It would have been equally acceptable to have performed the calculation using duration rather than DV01, and value amounts (so many dollars' worth of a bond) rather than nominal amounts. Recall that duration is risk per unit worth whereas DV01 is per unit nominal.

The trade is neutral to a parallel move in the curve, but a non-parallel move will cause profit or loss. If the yield of the 10-year decreases faster (or increases slower) than the yield of the 3-year, then the trade will be profitable; if the 10-year yield increases relative to the 3-year, there will be a loss.

A flattener generates cash

So the trade entails buying $100 nominal of the 2009 at a cost, including accrued interest of $99.87, and selling $276.72 nominal of the 2002 for $280.85, thus realising $180.98 of cash overall. And hence buying the $100 nominal of the 10-year and selling a *duration-weighted* amount of the 3-year generates $180.98 in cash.

If short-term interest rates are very high, say 20% as an extreme example, then this trade looks very attractive. But if short-term rates are low, then the low return from depositing the $180.98 reduces the attractiveness of the trade.

This puzzle over short-term rates is related to a second difficulty. The trade entails buying 10-years and selling 3-years. This is easy enough for an investor who already owns the 3-year, but what about one who doesn't? The answer to both of these puzzles lies in the use of repo.

A forward flattener

Recall that a repo transaction is just a collateralised deposit between two parties. One party lends the other cash; the other lends the one a bond. If the bond is an uninteresting bond, not in particular demand, then the repo rate, the interest rate on the deposit, will closely follow the appropriate IBOR, minus some amount because of the improved creditworthiness of the deposit. But if the bond is in particular demand, then the lender of the bond will be paid for lending this desirable bond. The form of this payment will be that the lender of the bond will borrow money at a lower rate of interest.

As of close of business on 14 October, these three bonds, the 3-, 5- and 10-year, had 3-month repo rates of 5.3%, 4.1% and 2.6%. Note the very low repo rate on the 10-year: a holder of this bond could borrow money for 3 months at only 2.6%. At the time, 3-month US Treasury general collateral (GC) rates were 5.36%, so a holder of the 10-year could borrow 3-month money 276bp cheaper than could a holder of an uninteresting US Treasury.

Consider the position of a trader who starts with an empty book; that is, without outstanding positions. If this trader were to buy the 10-year, the trader would need to borrow money to do so. And the cheapest way to borrow money is to use the same 10-year Treasury as collateral. If we assume that the borrowing is for 3 months, then the trader would be borrowing at the 10-year's 3-month repo rate of 2.6%.

Clearly, if the price increases greatly over that 3 months, the buyer of the bond will make a profit; and if the price falls far, a loss. There is a breakeven point, and this is the *forward price* of the bond. As in Chapter 1, the forward is the breakeven price (and hence the breakeven yield) implied by the market, to some future *horizon date*. The calculation of that breakeven must use the cost of borrowing the money to acquire the position.

So let us turn again to Bloomberg, this time to calculate the 3-month forward price of the 10-year, which is 98.01, a yield of 6.279%. Note that the forward yield is +12.6bp above the spot yield. So on 14 October 1999 the market was pricing that the yield of the 6% Aug 2009 would increase by 12.6bp over the following 3 months. The same calculation can be done for the 3-year, the 6.25% Aug 2002. Using the 3-month repo rate of 5.3%, the forward yield is 6.034%, 6.3bp over spot.

So the spot steepness of 3s10s is 18.2bp, but the 3-month forward steepness is 6.279% − 6.034% = 24.5bp, just over 6bp steeper than the spot steepness.

What happens if nothing happens?

We said that the correct hedge ratio for the 3s10s flattener was −$276.72 to $100, and if the trade were so weighted, then no change in the yield spread should cause no change in the profit or loss. Then we said that the forward steepness, i.e. the breakeven zero-P&L value, was just over 6bp steeper than the spot steepness. This might appear to be paradoxical, but in fact there is no paradox. Let us say that the trader buys 10s and sells 3s, using this duration-weighted ratio, and an hour or so later unwinds the trade. In this case, if the curve doesn't move, the profit will be zero. If the curve flattens there will be profit; if it steepens there will be loss.

But if the trade is held, rather than quickly unwound, there is *carry*, that is, a profit or loss from the passage of time. We can calculate the carry by hand, at least approximately. The 10-year bond has been bought and it yields 6.153%. The money to buy this bond has been borrowed at 2.6%. Lending at a high rate and borrowing at a low rate means that we're making money at a rate of about 344¢ per year. In performing this calculation, recall that the bond yield is quoted semi-annual but the repo is quoted quarterly. The trader has sold the 3-year, which yields 5.971%, and the proceeds from this sale are on deposit at 5.3%. This is losing the trader 55¢ per year per $100 value of the 3-year, so on $280.85 value costs 154¢ per year.

As time passes, if nothing happens, the trade makes 190¢ per year. This 190¢ gives a little protection; over three months it is worth 49¢, and 49¢ on $100 of the 10-year is equivalent to a little over 6bp. So the flattening trade only starts to lose money if the curve steepens by more than this number of basis points. This type of approximate forward calculation should be second nature to an experienced fixed-income trader or analyst.

Weighting the forward flattener

We have already shown that our 3s10s curve trade should be weighted using $276.72 of the 3-year for each $100 of the 10-year. However, if the curve trade is to be done 3 months forward, then allowance should be made for the interest-rate risk in the repo transactions.

There is an alternative way to see this. Imagine instead that our curve trade was between 1- and 2-year bonds. Per unit change in yield, the 2-year moves almost twice as fast as the 1-year, so the ratio would be almost 2-to-1 (trading more of the shorter bond). If this trade were performed 6 months forward, then the trade would be of a 6-month bond against an 18-month bond: the ratio would be nearer 3-to-1.

There are two methods of calculating the correct ratio for a forward flattener: one uses the DV01s of the forward bonds, and the other uses the DV01s of the spot bonds and the DV01s of the repo transactions. These methods give almost identical results; the point is that a forward trade will need different weights to a spot trade.

A barbell

We have looked in detail at a yield-curve-flattening trade. Let us now look briefly at another frequently seen class of trade, the *barbell*, sometimes called a *butterfly*. Consider the position of a pension fund which holds a particular bond that has recently become expensive to its neighbours (to other bonds with nearby maturities). The fund wants to sell its holding. However, the fund does not want to change the amount of money it has invested, nor does it wish to change its market exposure (the DV01 of its port-folio).

The natural course of action would be to switch its holding of this bond into two other bonds, one shorter and one longer. The amounts of the two destination bonds would be chosen so as to satisfy two conditions. First, their total value must be the same as the value of the bond being sold, which keeps constant the amount of money being invested. The second condition is that the total DV01 must be kept constant. There are two unknowns and two conditions, and hence there will be a solution. The two unknowns are the amounts of the two destination bonds, and the two condi-tions are constant money and constant risk per unit change in yield.

This is known as a cash-neutral duration-neutral barbell, and it is frequently used by *real-money* investors such as pension funds and insurers. However, there are numerous others ways to weight a barbell—a list of their rationales is beyond the scope of this book. The opposite trade, in which an investor sells the two wings to buy the centre, is a *reverse barbell*.

Carry and slide

For many trades it is natural to ask how much profit or loss would be made if nothing happened. This is known as *carry*, and there are at least three slightly different meanings in common usage.

Carry can mean the profit or loss that results from the passage of time, assuming prices remain unchanged. For example, consider a 2-year bond paying 8% annually, currently costing 103.667 and thus yielding 6%. Also assume that the 1-day repo rate is 5%. If the clean price of the bond remains constant, then in 1 day the dirty price increases by the accrued interest at a rate of 8% per annum, or 2.19¢ per day. The borrowing costs 5% per 100 of cash, and thus 1.44¢ per day per 100 nominal (allowing for the correct method of quoting money-market yields). So if clean prices remain unchanged, holding this bond makes 0.75¢ per day; this is the carry.

Carry can also mean the profit or loss that results from the passage of time, assuming that yields rather than prices remain unchanged. In this case it is easier to do the sums on 100 value rather than 100 nominal: the bond returns 6% per day (because this is the meaning of yield) and the funding costs 5% per day. The difference is about 0.76% per annum (not quite 1% because the yields are quoted in different conventions), so the carry is 0.207¢ per day per 100 value, or 0.215¢ per day per 100 nominal.

Alternatively, carry can mean the profit or loss that results from the passage of time, assuming that the yield curve remains unchanged. To illustrate this, let us assume a longer passage of time, say 3 months. The unchanged-yield version of carry would assume that, in 3 months, the then 1.75-year yield equals today's 2-year yield. If instead we assume that the yield curve remains unchanged, then we must assume that, in 3 months, the 1.75-year yield equals today's 1.75-year yield. This type of carry is not always easy to calculate, especially if today there isn't a suitable bond with exactly 1.75 years to maturity. The term *slide* ignores the cost of funding, and just refers to the difference between unchanged yields and the unchanged yield curve. If, for example, the 1.75-year bond now yields 5.87%, compared to the 2-year's 6%, then the slide would be 13bp over 3 months or 1bp per week, equal to 1.9¢ per week.

Summary

- Yields are not always quoted with the same compounding frequency; if yields are to be compared, it may be necessary to convert them to a matching type.
- Duration and DV01 measure the sensitivity of a bond or portfolio to a 0.01% move in yields; duration is per 100 worth, DV01 is per 100 nominal.
- Macaulay duration is the risk per 100 worth per change in the continuously compounded yield; modified duration is per change in the conventionally quoted yield.
- With yield and maturity held constant, a higher coupon will increase DV01 but reduce duration.
- Duration-weighted trades may produce or require cash.
- Forward yield-curve trades require repo; if the trade produces or requires cash, repo makes transparent the effect on the trade of the cash deposit or borrowing.
- Three-bond trades are called barbells; they are often weighted so as to be duration- and cash-neutral.
- Carry and slide describe what happens if nothing changes, though the term 'nothing' is somewhat ambiguous.

Chapter 13

Bond futures

Introduction

The interest-rate markets exist to allow borrowers to raise funds and investors to purchase assets. They allow the various types of interest rate and credit risks to be repackaged into a form that someone is willing to hold. For the most part, the instruments that are traded are well designed for their purpose. Some of these instruments are complicated but their complications are necessary, perhaps to make them into a better hedge for something else, or to reduce credit risk, or for some other need.

Bond futures are a partial exception to this. Their complications exist for a purpose, but at least to this author, they do not seem optimally designed for that purpose. Indeed, the specification of the bond contract seems to resemble that of an agricultural contract, perhaps because they were first listed on an exchange that then traded agricultural contracts. Still, that's history. Bond futures exist and are very important, so they must be described as they are, rather than as the author believes they should be. But readers are warned that bond futures are complicated instruments.

Specification

Just like any other futures contract, a bond future is a derivative, listed on an exchange. Both buyer and seller pay a good-faith deposit, known as initial margin, and as the price moves about this is topped up or down with variation margin. At delivery the short delivers and receives money from the long via the clearing house.

What is deliverable, and how much is paid for it? Let us use as an example the US 10-year Note contract, listed on the Chicago Board of Trade. The deliverables are

> U.S. Treasury notes maturing at least $6\frac{1}{2}$ years, but not more than 10 years, from the first day of the delivery month.

Note that many different bonds are deliverable. This is not a future on one particular security, with a particular coupon and maturing on a particular date. This is a future on a basket of US Treasuries. This is for a reason. If the future were on a single UST, it would be possible for a single market player to buy the whole security and squeeze the price. This is less easy with a large delivery basket. If one bond is squeezed and becomes unnaturally expensive, the shorts will choose to deliver a different cheaper bond.

However, what has been described so far isn't enough. Consider two USTs, both with 8 years to maturity, one paying a nominal coupon of 5%, one of 7.5%. At 6% yields the first costs 93.72, and the second 109.42. If the 5% were squeezed so that it cost 109.42, it would yield only 3.63%. So, unless there is some mechanism to deal with the fact that different bonds have different coupons, the low-coupon bonds would always be cheapest to deliver. That is why there is such a mechanism; it is called a *conversion factor*.

> The invoice price equals the futures settlement price times a conversion factor plus accrued interest.

So, at delivery, the short is not paid the last price of the future. The short is paid the last traded price times a conversion factor plus accrued interest. The conversion factor for high-coupon bonds is above 1, and the conversion factor for low-coupon bonds is below 1. In this way, delivery of high-coupon bonds is rewarded and delivery of low-coupon bonds penalised. The conversion factors are calculated by an easy formula:

> The conversion factor is the price of the delivered note ($1 par value) to yield 6 percent.

We shall soon see that this formula has significant implications.

For the US Treasury contract, the contract size is $100,000. During the delivery month the short must deliver $100,000 nominal of a deliverable security. The size of the contract also determines the scale of the variation margin, in that a $1 price change (say from $100 to $101) causes $1000 of variation margin to be paid or received.

Delivery day

The first futures contracts were on agricultural goods, such as wheat. With these contracts, the short physically delivers the produce to an exchange-approved warehouse. This delivery necessitates using ports or roads or railways, loading and unloading equipment, and other such infrastructure.

Were all the shorts to deliver simultaneously, at the same time as all the longs were collecting, there would be gridlock. To prevent this, the specification of most agricultural contracts allows delivery on many different days. CBoT listed the first US Treasury Bond contracts in 1976. The agricultural contracts then listed on CBoT allowed delivery on any day in the delivery month, and the US Treasury Bond future inherited the rule allowing delivery on any day of the month.

The second government bond contract to be listed was on long-dated British gilts, and it inherited the same agricultural-style rule from the Bond contract, as did the US futures on shorter-dated USTs. But when futures on Bunds, German government debt, were being listed in London in 1987, it was realised that it was unnecessary to have multiple delivery days. Government bonds settle electronically, and one can deliver a billion as easily as a million, without any chance of gridlock. So futures on Bunds have a single delivery day. This rule has been inherited by other bond contracts listed since.

The delivery process

The details of the delivery process vary from exchange to exchange and from contract to contract, but similar principles underlie each one. For simplicity, let us start with a contract that has a single delivery day:

1. Trading continues until a predetermined time on the last trading day.
2. The exchange calculates the final price: either the price of the last trade, or the average of the prices of the trades over the last few minutes.
3. Usually, most positions in this contract month will have been closed before trading ceases, but some will remain. Each remaining short must inform the clearing house of which bond is going to be delivered.
4. The longs will be *assigned* deliveries. If all the shorts say that they will deliver the same bond, then each long will be assigned that bond. But if two or more different bonds are being delivered, which long gets which bond will be chosen randomly.
5. Each long now knows how much money must be paid: final price times conversion factor for that bond, plus accrued interest.
6. On delivery day itself, each short delivers to the clearing house the bonds that it has promised to deliver; these are passed through to the longs, who pay the required cash.

The procedure for contracts with multiple delivery days is similar, except that the exchange must calculate a settlement price on many different days, and on every day except the last, each short might or might not choose to deliver.

For both types, the short chooses which bond to deliver. This is crucial. But which bond will the short choose to deliver? The short will choose to deliver whichever bond is *cheapest to deliver* (CTD). This will depend on the level of yields and the shape of the yield curve. Because bond futures are such heavily traded instruments, CTD dynamics is very important to the bond markets, and that is our next topic.

Cheapest to deliver: at par

On delivery day, the short must deliver one of the deliverables. The short will always want to deliver the CTD. Note that if the short already owns a different deliverable, the short can make a profit by selling the bond that is more expensive to deliver, buying and then delivering the CTD.

For simplicity, let us concentrate on a contract with a single delivery day. As our example we shall take the Bund contract, listed on Eurex, a Frankfurt-based futures exchange. The bonds deliverable into this contract are

German Federal Bonds (Bundesanleihen) with a remaining term upon delivery of $8\frac{1}{2}$ to $10\frac{1}{2}$ years

As with the US contract, the invoice price equals the futures settlement price multiplied by a conversion factor, plus accrued interest, and the conversion factor is the price of €1 of the delivered bond assuming that it yields 6%. The size of the contract is €100,000.

Let us start with the easiest situation: imagine there are only a few moments until trading ceases, the contract currently costs 100 exactly, and each of the deliverable Bunds yields exactly 6%. Then each of these deliverables would be exactly equally cheap to deliver. Were an investor to buy €100,000 nominal of any one of the deliverables, and sell against that one contract, the investor would exactly break even.

Why? Because in delivering that bond, the investor would be paid the future's settlement price (which we know to be 100) times the conversion factor (the clean price of the bond assuming that it yields 6%, divided by 100), plus the accrued interest. So whichever bond were bought and delivered, the investor would exactly break even. Recall that this is the whole purpose of the conversion factors: they make bonds with very different coupons much nearer to being equally cheap to deliver.

Also observe that, if it is the last trading day, and each deliverable bond yields 6%, then the contract must cost 100. This is because, if it cost more than 100, an investor could buy a deliverable, sell the contract and generate a guaranteed profit. And if the contract cost less than 100, an investor could buy this contract and sell whichever bond was delivered, again for a guaranteed profit.

Cheapest to deliver: far from par

So we now know that if each of the deliverables yields 6%, they must all be equally cheap to deliver. But what if their prices are higher and each yields 5%? In this case the CTD must be the bond that has increased least in price.

Recall that duration describes the relative speed of price and yield movements. For any given yield change, the price of a bond with a smaller duration will change by a smaller percentage than the price of a bond with a larger duration. So, of the deliverables, the bond with the shortest duration will be the bond that has increased in price by the least. And because even the CTD has increased in price, albeit by less than the others, the contract would cost substantially more than par. This example is typical of a general rule. If a bond contract is a long way above par, the CTD will typically be the shortest of the deliverable bonds.

And what if all the deliverables yield 7%? If they all yielded 6%, they would be equally cheap to deliver. So if they yield 7%, the CTD must be the bond whose price has fallen furthest. All the bonds have had the same change in yield, so it must be the bond with the longest duration that has fallen furthest in price. Therefore, if a bond contract is a long way below par, the longest bond will typically be the CTD.

To summarise, if the price of a bond future is above par then the CTD tends to be the shortest deliverable; if the price is below par then the CTD tends to be the longest deliverable.

CTD calculations before delivery

All of this assumed that delivery was imminent. But if delivery is not imminent, the calculation becomes much more involved. It starts by observing the current prices and repo rates for each of the deliverables, and then calculating their prices forward to the delivery day.

One of the forward prices, after adjustment for the conversion factor, is the lowest. This bond is currently CTD. A buyer of the futures contract may well be delivered this bond. However, there is a risk that, during the time to delivery, some other bond becomes cheaper to deliver. And hence the contract should trade even cheaper than the cheapest of the conversion-factor-adjusted forward prices.

For each bond the difference between the adjusted forward price of a bond and the price of the future is known as the *basis net of carry* (BNOC) for that bond. The BNOC for the CTD represents the price of the seller's option to choose which bond to deliver; the price of the delivery option is actively traded.

Futures on gilts and Treasuries allow the short an additional choice: as well as choosing which bond to deliver, the short may choose on which day in the delivery month it is delivered. But even without this timing option, valuation of the basis (of the delivery option) is a very complicated task.

Note that this is our third use of the word 'basis'. It can refer to a basis point, a unit of 0.01%; to a basis swap, a swap in which floating payments in one currency are exchanged for floating in another currency; and to the adjusted forward price of a deliver-able relative to that of the future.

Delivery tail

There is another complication on bond futures, called the delivery tail. To explain this we revert to our first example of a futures contract, the COMEX gold contract. This contract has a size of 100 troy ounces, so a $1 move in the price (quoted per troy ounce) causes a $100 move in variation margin per contract. This rela-tionship is exact. But when we quoted the specification of the COMEX gold contract in Chapter 3, we omitted the following detail. While the variation margin works as if the contract has an underlying of exactly 100 troy ounces, when it comes to deliv-ery the seller is actually allowed up to 5% slippage:

the seller must deliver 100 troy ounces (±5%) of refined gold, ...

What would happen if the seller delivered 95 troy ounces? When a contract ceases trading, the exchange on which it is traded declares a final price. In the example from Chapter 3 this would be $278/oz. Variation margin up to this value is paid. Delivery then takes place, at this price per troy ounce. So if a seller delivered 95 troy ounces, that seller would be paid 95 × $278 = $26,410. As with the bond futures, the amount that is paid by the long depends on what is delivered.

Note that both parties have experienced a change in their risk. Just before the delivery price was determined, a $1 increase in the price of gold made the owner of the contract $100 richer. So the owner of the contract was in effect long 100 troy ounces. And likewise, the seller was short 100 oz. But then the final delivery price is determined, and the seller's delivery notice says that only 95 oz are to be delivered. The position of the trader who is long shrinks by 5% to 95 oz. To maintain the same effective exposure, the person with the long position would have to buy a little extra gold. Likewise, the seller's short position has shrunk, and to ensure that the effective exposure is the same after delivery as before delivery, the seller would have to sell a little more. This extra amount that needs to be bought or sold is known as the *delivery tail*.

In bond futures, a delivery tail can be caused by the conversion factor. If the conversion factor of the delivered bond is greater than 1, then both the long and short positions increase in size over delivery. If it is less than 1, both positions become a little smaller. Usually, which bond is CTD is known well before the delivery day. And hence both longs and shorts know the conversion factor of the bond that will be delivered. If this conversion factor is above 1, then the longs would benefit from an artificially low exchange delivery settlement price (EDSP), whereas the shorts would like the EDSP to be artificially high. Because of these incentives, sometimes the price action can be somewhat anomalous as a contract expires.

Summary

- A bond future has multiple deliverable bonds.
- The price paid is the final price of the contract multiplied by a conversion factor.
- The short will choose to deliver whichever bond is the cheapest to deliver (CTD).
- If the price of a bond future is below par, the CTD tends to be the longest deliverable; if the price is above par, it tends to be the shortest deliverable.
- The price of the delivery option is the BNOC of the CTD; valuation of this is complicated.
- The risk of both longs and shorts can change over delivery.

Chapter 14

Basic fixed-income arithmetic

Some understanding of fixed-income arithmetic is useful to those working in financial markets. Some of this relates to market conventions, and some to back-of-the-envelope calculations about prices and yields. We start with market conventions.

The proportion of a year

Let us imagine that a bank is borrowing €100 from Wednesday 17 August 2011 to Friday 17 February 2012, at a rate of 8%. Clearly the interest cost will be €100 × 8% × p, where p is the proportion of a year that lies between these dates. So what proportion of a year is this?

One might reasonably argue that it is 0.5 years exactly, as 17 August to 17 February is 6 months. Or one might argue that this is 184 days and that most years contain 365 days, so this proportion is

$$184/385 \approx 0.504109589 \text{ year}$$

Alternatively one might argue that 48 days of this period lie in a leap year, so in this period the weighted average length of a year is

$$(48 \times 366 + 136 \times 365)/184 \approx 365.260869565 \text{ days}$$

and the proportion of a year is

$$184/365.260869565 \approx 0.5037495536$$

Indeed, one could devise other formulae. Whichever formula is to be used would have to be agreed between the parties in advance. And it doesn't really matter which formula is used:

$$8\% \text{ for } 0.5 \text{ years}$$

is equivalent to

$$7.9347826\% \text{ for } 0.504109589 \text{ years}$$

is equivalent to

$$7.940453686\% \text{ for } 0.5037495536 \text{ years}$$

So, provided that the parties agree on a particular formula for calculating the proportion of a year, the price can subsequently take the strain

One could even use a nonsensical formula such as dividing the actual number of days in the period by 360, known as *Act/360*. This would be manifestly ridiculous, but nonetheless has managed to become the money-market convention for several large currencies. It is obviously nonsense—no year has 360 days—but that doesn't matter, because the market price will compensate for the silly convention.

For example, 4.5% when quoted Act/360 is the same as 4.5625% quoted Act/365. To be specific, the money markets in USD, JPY, EUR and other continental European currencies use Act/360; those in GBP and ZAR use Act/365. When comparing sterling and euro money-market interest rates, it is important to know that they might be quoted differently.

Likewise, the calculation of accrued interest for a bond relies on knowing what proportion of the coupon period has passed. Again, each market has its own convention, and some of these conventions are less than sensible. It doesn't matter: the price paid, the dirty price, equals the quoted clean price plus the accrued. If the accrued is artificially low, whatever that may mean, then a higher clean price can compensate.

Let us now move on to some rough-and-ready calculations.

Yield to price and price to yield

We have an 8% 10-year bond costing 115. What is the yield? Well, we know that if this bond cost 100, it would yield 8%. We also know that a 10-year bond has a duration of about 7.5, and hence a 15-point move in the price is roughly equivalent to a 2% move in the yield. So this bond yields about 6%.

The actual answer? If the bond pays annually, and has an annual-quoted yield, then the actual answer is 5.965%. If both are semi-annual, the answer is 5.985%.

This calculation required the duration. As approximations, a 2-year bond has a duration of just under 2 years, a 5-year of between 4 and 4.5 (call it 4.25), a 10-year of between 7 and 8 (call it 7.5), a 20-year of between 10 and 13, and a 30-year of 12 to 17.

Semi to annual: halve and square

Let us assume that a US Treasury yields 6%, and that a similar-duration Swiss government bond yields 4%. What is the yield differential? Recall that US Treasury yields are quoted semi-annual, most European bonds are quoted annual. Because of the different conventions, before subtraction the yields should be converted into a common form.

Fortunately, there is a quick mathematical rule that allows conversion of semi-annual yields to annual yields: halve and square. The Treasury yields 6%: halve this number to get 3, square it to get 9, and that is the number of basis points to add. So 6% semi-annual is 6.09% annual, and the yield differential is thus 209bp.

Forward yield

Assume that we have a 6% 10-year bond trading at a price of 100; its 3-month repo rate is 4%. What is the bond's forward price and what is its forward yield? Start by observing that this bond yields 2% more than its repo rate. So over a quarter of a year, the holder makes a quarter of 2%, or 50¢. Thus the forward price is about 99.50. This bond has a duration of 7.5, so 50¢ is equivalent to 6.66bp. The forward yield is therefore close to 6.07%.

Forward asset swap

Forward asset swaps can be estimated in a similar manner. Assume that a 5-year bond is trading at swaps − 75bp but that its 6-month repo rate is only 25bp less than Libor. This bond is therefore expensive to fund; its yield is Libor − 75bp but borrowing against the bond is 50bp dearer than this. The 50bp differential for 6 months is worth 25¢. On a 5-year bond, with a duration of just over 4 years, 25¢ is about 5.9bp. The funding was expensive, so breakeven will only be achieved if the bond rallies. The breakeven (or forward) asset swap is therefore about −80.9bp.

Summary

- Market conventions aren't always sensible, but the price can always take the strain.
- It is useful to know a bond's duration.
- It is easy to calculate yields and relative yields forward to a horizon: calculate the carry to that date in cents then convert back to basis points.

Index